Rev. R. T. Williams, D. D.

SANCTIFICATION

The Experience and The Ethics

By

DR. R. T. WILLIAMS, D. D.

NAZARENE PUBLISHING HOUSE
2923 Troost Ave., Kansas City, Mo.

FOREWORD

This little volume is published not because the world needs more books. Its object is two-fold, 1st is an endeavor to answer some uncharitable and also some honest criticisms against those who profess the experience of full salvation. 2nd it is written with a sincere desire to aid those who possess a pure heart and are trying to live a life consistent with their testimony.

What is to follow is not an apology for the doctrine of holiness nor for those who claim such experience. No apology is necessary. The doctrines of the Bible need no defense.

There is a deep conviction in the heart of the writer that proper distinction has not been made between the experience of holiness and the ethics of holiness in the preaching and writings on this subject. That is why we have ventured to publish this book.

If we can cheer some honest, conscientious person in his fight to give to his neighbors and friends an ethical life that will harmonize with that glorious divine image he has within his soul, our effort will be well worth while.

It is always a consolation to know that God looketh upon the heart, the motives, rather than upon the outward appearance. This however

14151

does not justify anyone in being careless of his ethics. We need wisdom or ethical knowledge, which will form right relationships—relationships that are profitable and pleasing.

In this there is room for improvement with us all. The Bible urges us to seek and pray for more wisdom that we may better know how to be real examples of believers. Seeing the good works and ethical life of God's children, the world will be more inclined to glorify our Father in heaven. Being a Christian and living like Christ is the greatest achievement possible.

This little book is an endeavor to express in a small way the heart-throb and passion of the writer's soul to thus achieve, and encourage others in their sincere effort to do likewise.

R. T. W.

CONTENTS

Sanctification—The Experience and The Ethics

CHAPTER ONE

Sanctification

Sanctification is one of the sacred and fundamental doctrines of the Bible and of the Christian church. It has occupied a place of prominence in the writings and discussions of the leading theologians and Christian teachers for generations. No church or individual advocate of Bible truth can view this doctrine with indifference and unconcern. It commands a place of respect at the hands of all believers in the Word of God. Indeed, it would be difficult for any conscientious student of Divine Revelation to study systematically the teachings of the world's outstanding scholars without giving this truth its rightful place in thought and discussion. Every student of Church history and of the doctrines of the Christian church from its origin, knows full well that sanctification has been placed in some kind of setting with the other doctrines of the church, and that it must be considered if one is to have a right understanding of the doctrines of Christianity.

9

The doctrine of Sanctification is scriptural. The Bible clearly and unmistakably teaches this truth. It is found in the types of the Old Testament and is definitely stated in the teachings and doctrines of the New Testament. No intelligent reader can study the biography of the prophets, the ceremonies and types and shadows of the old dispensation, the statements of Jesus in the Gospels, and the doctrines of Paul in the epistles to the churches without admitting that the Bible presents sanctification in the great scheme of salvation. At another place in this chapter we shall present statements and definitions of outstanding scholars and also quotations from the Word of God to establish the fact that sanctification is a doctrine of both the Church and of the Bible.

Again, the doctrine of sanctification is perfectly logical. When one accepts as true the story of the fall of man, his moral corruption, and his inherited depravity, sanctification must become a logical sequence in his system of belief. There is no escape from this conclusion. A right definition of sin, and a scriptural understanding of the sin question, make almost certain our belief concerning all other Bible doctrines. A wrong conception of sin paves the way for a misunderstanding and a wrong interpretation of the entire Word of God. Find a man who has a correct view of sin and you will find it easy to indoctrinate him in other truths of the Bible.

It has always been recognized that the philosophy of salvation is the most beautiful ever presented to the mind of man. The story of the fall and the redemption of man through Jesus Christ is the most romantic, the most gripping, the most fascinating ever related from a public platform or read from a book. How glorious was man in his original state! What a tragedy is related in his fall! What indescribable love was manifested by the Father in His passion and effort to restore man to moral rectitude and to divine favor! Let one accept the fact that man was originally pure, that he fell, that he sinned, that he became morally corrupt through his fall, that he is both guilty and impure, then the logic of regeneration and sanctification as well becomes both irresistible and beautiful. Sanctification is unanswerably logical and gloriously attractive.

At this point it would be well to call the reader's attention to the glorious work of regeneration, in order that a better understanding of the truth of sanctification might be possible. It really becomes necessary in order to prepare the

way for what follows in the discussion of sanctification.

Three facts make regeneration—or conversion or the new birth—a necessity (we take the
liberty to use the terms synonymously), namely:
first, spiritual death; *second*, transgression, or
sins committed; *third*, acquired pollution.

In regeneration these three facts are met in
full and the conditions that make regeneration
necessary are removed. *First*, spiritual death is
replaced by a new divine life. *Second*, the sins
one has committed are forgiven him; and *third*,
he is cleansed from the pollutions acquired
through the transgression of the law. He was
once dead, now he is alive. He was once guilty,
now he is forgiven. He had acquired pollution
by his acts of transgression; he is now cleansed
of this pollution. What a wonderful work! All
will readily admit that such a change is the need
of every individual in the world that has not
already received such a work of divine grace.
What a change it would bring to the world if all
men had this transformation of mind, of character, and of life! Think of the glory of having
the soul pass from death unto life! Think of
the joy of having one's sins forgiven him! Think
of the inner peace and consolation resulting from
the fact that the pollution acquired through

breaking the laws of God has been washed away!

John Wesley makes the following statement concerning regeneration: "The new birth is that great change which God works in the soul when He brings it into life; when He raises from the death of sin to the life of righteousness. It is the change wrought in the whole soul by the Almighty Spirit of God when it is created anew in Christ Jesus; when it is renewed after the image of God in righteousness and true holiness."

Dr. Hanna says: "Regeneration is the mighty change in man, wrought by the Holy Spirit, by which the dominion which sin had over him in his natural state, and which he deplores and struggles against in his penitent state, is broken and demolished; so that with full choice of will and the energy of right assertion he serves God freely and runs in the way of His commandments."

Regeneration has been defined by one as an ingeneration of divine life; a sudden process by which man passes from spiritual death to a spiritual life through the quickening power of God's Holy Spirit. As has been stated, in regeneration one passes from a state of death to a state of spiritual life; from a state of guilt to a state of "forgiveness;" from a state of pollution—that is, the pollution acquired by his own acts of disobedience against the laws of God—to a state of conscious cleansing; that is, a cleansing from acquired pollution. Thus regeneration has cleansing, not from the moral corruption inherited through the fall, but cleansing from that moral pollution acquired by his own acts of disobedience. Regeneration, or conversion, used in a broad sense, may be defined, therefore, as the act of the Holy Spirit in answer to faith by which spiritual life is imparted to a dead soul, his sins are freely forgiven him, and the moral corruption accumulated through his sins taken away. The man stands as a new creature in Christ Jesus; old things have passed away and all things become new. He recognizes that he is no longer a friend to the world but God's child, separated from all that is evil and committed to obedience to God's holy commandments.

Inherited depravity, or that corruption of moral nature passed down to a man through his birth, is not destroyed at conversion, or cleansed away in regeneration. It is mastered, conquered, but not annihilated. This fact is clearly taught by the Bible and can be proven easily by the testimony and experiences of those who have been converted and have lived long enough after conversion to experience the stirrings of a nature within them that their very soul and better judgment abhor. Who has not felt anger or pride or malice or some other unholy temper or passion within his bosom since that glorious day of his conversion? What person would to-day stand and testify that he had not discovered within himself a nature unlike Christ, one that he was forced to fight with desperation to keep it from mastering him and forcing him to some act that would mar his influence and grieve his Lord? Yea, since he passed from death unto life has he not had such experience?

The writer found one person in his travels who gave testimony that he had never had such stirrings since conversion but he did not maintain his position very long. The wife of this dear man came to the defense of the truth when she looked her cultured and highly educated husband in the face and said, "How dare you say you have not had unholy feelings in your heart since you first began to serve God! I have detected such spirit in you myself many times." This very fine, high class gentleman leaned back in his chair and looked toward the ceiling, saying, "It is probable that I am wrong. Perhaps I am mistaken." This was an honest man. He was a Christian, but he had an enemy within him that disturbed his peace; and so has every converted man who has not gone on to the glorious experience of sanctification. Sanctification answers the need of every man at this point in his struggle against the fallen nature within him in his great soul-passion for Christ's likeness.

Regeneration and sanctification both deal primarily with the sin question. That is why they are called the first and second blessings or works of grace. There are many blessings in Christian experience and Christian life, but there are two blessings that are called the first and second blessings. This is due to the fact that these two specific blessings deal with the question of sin. The one deals primarily with what we do, the other primarily with what we are. It would not be altogether correct to say that regeneration deals with the act alone. We have already stated that regeneration deals with sins committed, with spiritual death, and with acquired pollution. Neither would it be quite correct to assert that sanctification deals only with our inner state. This is true primarily, but indirectly it deals with our ethics because of the fact that our inner state makes it easier or harder for us to live right externally.

It appears to the writer that the question that lies at the very heart of justification is one of broken law, one of guilt, one of transgression. This is the factor that largely enters into the seeking of Christ on the part of a sinner. The fact of his guilt, of his condemnation, of the transgression of the law of a righteous and just God is the thing that drives him to seek forgiveness at the hands of Jesus Christ.

Primarily sanctification has to do with man's inner nature or condition, as justification does with his outer conduct. In a word, when a man is converted he is forgiven and restored to favor with God. The power of sin is broken, "the old man" of sin is conquered, the power of the new life within him is greater than the power of a fallen nature. This inherited bias, or "prone to wander," this inner opposition to the law of God is not destroyed, it is conquered in regeneration. It is destroyed, absolutely annihilated, in sanctification.

Here is the great battle ground concerning holiness. The question is simply this, is sin destroyed in the act of sanctification or not? This is the question on which turns all belief in sanctification. It is folly to try to pass as a believer in holiness and at the same time question its doctrine of eradication. There can not be such a thing as holiness in its final analysis without the eradication of sin. Holiness and suppression are incompatible terms. "The old man" and counteraction make a pale and sickly kind of holiness doctrine. It is holiness and eradication or holiness not at all. Some tell us that they believe in the positive side of holiness, but not in the negative side. That is, they believe that a man can be filled with the Holy Spirit but can not be delivered instantaneously in this life from all sin. It seems strange that God could fill and satisfy the heart of man but at the same time not have the power to annihilate sin in his heart. If one does not believe in the eradication of sin in the heart he does not believe in holiness. His belief concerning eradication is the determining factor in his attitude toward the great doctrine of full salvation. This is the crux of the whole matter and it is useless to juggle words or become confused by hair-splitting theological discussions. Concerning holiness there is one question to settle, Can God destroy sin utterly, and does He do it in this life?

It is significant that men who quit the radical circle of holiness teaching usually justify themselves by saying that they have long doubted the eradication theory of sanctification. It is also significant that usually such persons make the change, not in the height of their glory and success, but when their popularity is beginning to wane. This change of mind is not announced while they are in some good position usually, but at such time as when the future looks rather dark to them. When once popularity begins to wane and he begins to get censorious and critical and feel that he is not rightly treated, that his talents are not fully appreciated, then it becomes quite easy to change his belief concerning eradication. It is quite easy to change one's theory to suit his experience. It is a dangerous thing to do, but this is often the case. It is always safe to bring up the experience to the standards of the Word of God when one finds "the old man" in his heart. He should cry out for his destruction instead of trying to defend himself by changing his opinions concerning the crucifixion of carnality. Can God destroy "the old man"? If He cannot and does not then the doctrine of sanctification can not be defended on the grounds of reason, logic, or the Word of God. If the Holy Ghost does destroy "the old man" in the act of sanctification, then the doctrine should be believed, accepted, and carried to the ends of the earth as a solution of man's problems and as his chief protection. A doctrine that lifts man to a glorious standard of righteousness of character and conduct is not to be despised.

Since we have attempted to define regeneration, it might be well to call the reader's attention to some definitions of sanctification. It would hardly be logical or worthwhile to defend a doctrine without stating just what one means by such a doctrine.

First, let us view some definitions given by a few of the world's great scholars and teachers. Mr. Webster says: "Sanctification: first, to make sacred and holy; to set apart to a holy, religious use; to consecrate by appropriate rights; to hallow. Second, to make free from sin; to cleanse from moral corruption and pollution; to purify. Sanctification; the act of making holy; the state of being sanctified or made holy. Theologically, the act of God's goodness by which the affections of man are purified, are alienated from sin and the world, and exalted to a supreme love of God; also the state of those being purified or sanctified."

The Standard Dictionary makes the following statement: "Sanctification: To make holy; render sacred or morally or spiritually pure; cleansed from sin. Sanctification is specifically, not theologically, the gracious work of the Holy Spirit, whereby the believer is freed from sin and exalted to holiness of heart and life."

John Wesley says: "Sanctification, in the proper sense, is an instantaneous deliverance from all sin, and includes an instantaneous power then given to cleave always to God."

The following is a definition given by Pope's Theology: "Sanctification in its beginnings, processes and final issue is the full eradication of sin itself, which, reigning in the unregenerate, co-exists with the new life in the regenerate, is abolished in the wholly sanctified."

Rev. Luther Lee defines sanctification thus: "Sanctification is that renewal of our fallen nature by the Holy Ghost, received through faith in Jesus Christ, whose blood of atonement has power to cleanse from all sin; whereby we are not only delivered from the guilt of sin, which is justification, but are washed entirely from its pollution, freed from its power, and are enabled, through grace, to love God with all our hearts, to walk in His holy commandments blameless."

The Methodist Catechism says: "Sanctification is that act of divine grace whereby we are made holy."

Dr. Steele says: "The act is that of removing impurity existing in the nature of one already born of the Spirit—the deliverance from sin as a tendency born with us."

Rev. Wm. McDonald makes these statements: "In regeneration, sin does not reign; in sanctification it does not exist. In regeneration, sin is suspended; in sanctification it is destroyed. In regeneration, irregular desires such as anger, pride, unbelief, envy, are subdued; in sanctification they are removed. Regeneration is salvation from the voluntary commission of sin; sanctification is salvation from the being of sin. Regeneration is the old man bound; sanctification is the old man cast out and spoiled of his goods. Regeneration is sanctification begun; entire sanctification is the work completed."

It would be possible for us to go on giving definition after definition, but we feel this is sufficient to convince the reader that sanctification is a doctrine and that it has special meaning. The statements given are all clear and the definitions have come from men who think, from men who not only know Christian doctrine but the Bible as well. These definitions indicate that sanctification deals primarily with the question of purifying the heart from inherited depravity; and it also includes the matter of dedicating one's life to God in consecration.

Sanctification is both human and divine. Man has always had a part in the application of the atonement of Jesus Christ to himself. Christ's death on the cross provisionally saved everybody but actually saved nobody except in the case of the irresponsible. The benefits of Christ's death are strictly individual. That is, each individual must make application for those

blessings purchased for him by the death of
Christ. These blessings are appropriated by the
voluntary act of the individual coming to Jesus
Christ. "Whosoever will" is the teaching of
God's Word. If man does not come to Christ
to accept His blessings, the merits of Christ will
have no meaning for him so far as salvation is
concerned. In order to be converted one must
do his part. He must repent and exercise faith
in Christ. In order to be sanctified one must do
his part. Thus it is evident that sanctification
has both the human element and the divine element. It is both consecration and purification.
These two elements combined constitute the
great truth of entire sanctification. Consecration is the human element, or man's part. "Sanctify yourselves therefore and be ye holy" says
the Word of God. In the strictest sense God can
not consecrate a man. Man must do this for
himself. God can call, urge, and insist; but in
the final analysis man must present himself to
God. He must make his own consecration vol-
untarily. God can and will accept such consecration and use the man thus consecrated for
the honor of His own name and the advance-
ment of His kingdom. The act of consecration
is man's part and constitutes the human element
in sanctification.

We could not stop here and be true to the teachings of the Word of God and the definitions given above. If consecration is sanctification or if sanctification is consecration and that only, then it is all purely human and God has little or nothing to do with it except to accept the work done by man. This position could never be justified nor defended. The writer of Hebrews says, "He that sanctifieth and they who are sanctified are all of one: for which cause he is not ashamed to call them brethren." Here we have the sanctifier, the sanctified, and the relation that exists between the sanctifier and the sanctified. If sanctification is consecration only, how could there be a sanctifier, unless that sanctifier is a man himself? This could not possibly harmonize with the text of scripture under consideration. Consecration is a part: it is the human element; but there is a divine side to this great truth. Paul prayed that the very God of peace might sanctify us wholly. He also says, "Husbands, love your wives, even as Christ also loved the church, and gave himself for it; that he might . . . cleanse it." It is evident from this statement that God Himself is the Sanctifier. This consecration is divinely accepted, the heart is cleansed from all unrighteousness, and man is enabled by the circumcision of his heart to love

God with his whole soul, mind, and strength. Man sanctifies himself through consecration. God sanctifies him by the baptism with the Holy Ghost and fire. In this the work is complete. Man's part is accomplished through consecration, and God's part is accomplished in purification. Man dedicates himself to the Lord and in answer to a living faith (this man) receives the baptism with the Holy Ghost and fire by which his heart is purified and he is filled with the love of God. The refining fire is sent through his heart and the whole nature is purified. What a glorious work! What a marvelous accomplishment! Man lays himself in submission at the feet of God. His all is accepted, he is made a vessel meet for the Master's use. What person could find fault with a perfect consecration? Who would dare state that there could be anything wrong in the consecration of every child of God to the Almighty? Who could find fault with cleansing for the human heart?

CHAPTER TWO

OBJECTIONS TO SANCTIFICATION CONSIDERED

Opposition to sanctification is a well known fact. This doctrine is the object of more criticism and ridicule than any other doctrine of the Bible except one, namely, the deity of Jesus Christ. The deity of Jesus today is receiving the united and determined attacks of all the enemies of Bible truth wherever they are to be found, whether in the church or outside of the church. The enemy of the Word of God knows full well that if he can blast at the foundation of belief in the deity of our Lord until this belief is thoroughly undermined in the thinking of the people, the whole superstructure of Christianity will crumble into ruins. In this case there would be nothing more to do, as the whole work of destruction would have been accomplished and Christianity be at an end. The Christian church would pass and heathenism would hold undisputed sway over all nations of the world.

Next to this truth, namely the deity of Jesus, sanctification has received more slurs, more ridicule, more direct attacks than any other truth believed and taught by the Christian church.

Much of this opposition has been due to misunderstanding. Unfavorable reports, rumors, and radical statements made by unwise teachers and leaders have contributed to this misunderstanding. Any sacred truth can be brought into disrepute by its own advocates if such truth is unwisely handled and presented. You will often find objections in the minds of fair and openhearted people because of things they have heard that misrepresented the truth, being presented by unwise teachers and leaders. A calm, open-minded, unprejudiced consideration of the definitions given by the best writers and theologists of the centuries along doctrinal lines will convince those who look with suspicion and fear upon sanctification that it is worthy of thorough investigation. No one should reach his conclusions through mere rumors, hearsay, or extreme fanatical expressions from unwise teachers.

Ignorance of the doctrine of sanctification has been the cause of much of the opposition that has been expressed against it. This situation can be greatly remedied both by the advocate of holiness and by the critic who examines the claims of this doctrine. Both should be more careful and cautious regarding this and all other truth.

Some of the opposition to sanctification is doubtless due to the strenuous demands made upon us by the doctrine. Humanity is usually ready to accept something offered, but is always slow to give up what is already possessed. There is little opposition to the positive side of holiness. All would like to have perfect love, greater power, more joy, or some other outstanding attraction, but few seemingly are willing to die to self and to sin. The multitudes that followed Jesus Christ were happy and contented as long as they could continue to hold what they had and receive something more; but one day the Master began to make demands upon them, saying they must deny themselves in order to follow Him.

Turning to His followers He said: "If any man will come after me he must do three things. *First*, he must deny himself; *second*, he must take up his cross; and *third*, he must follow me." It was the giving up of something one already had that was the determining factor in discipleship. Were they willing to give up their sins, to die to themselves, and to deny themselves?

That was the great question. Church members and professed Christians everywhere are always glad to seek power, or fire, or joy, or peace, or some desirable blessing; but they are not so willing to consent to die to themselves. Death is unpleasant. This is where the battle actually begins. Offer the world religion that it can take along with its sinful pleasures and the followers will be many; but when you ask men to die to sin and surrender their wills, to give up their own plans and their own ambitions and their own philosophy of life and take Jesus Christ and what He has to offer, you begin a battle that determines the outcome and the destiny of souls.

The religion that demands self-denial has never been popular and it never can be popular. If we could offer the world today a religion that could be possessed without interference with sinful pleasure, sinful appetites, sinful passions—a religion that would not conflict with the belief, the ideals, and the standards of human society —the multitudes would readily accept it. But a religion that comes into conflict with custom, ethics, and the pleasures of the human heart will immediately meet opposition. This is why it is difficult to get people to gather at the altar for prayer. They prefer to raise a hand, to sign a card, or to do something that is easy. For people to come forward in the presence of the crowds and get down on their knees in submission and humiliation before God brings on a moral conflict that is unpleasant. Men pull back from it until they are ready to pay the price of real discipleship. Anything that produces a moral conflict will work good in the salvation of men. A religion that does not produce a moral conflict is of no value. One of the evidences that the Bible is the Word of God is that its very presence forces men to accept or reject it, to take sides with it or take sides against it. Prayer is another fact that produces moral conflict and moral fight. This is why the mourner's bench, the old method of getting men to kneel down and then to pray, is of great value in the salvation of souls. Anything that will bring the will to an issue, that will cause the heart to submit to its God, will bring out the best there is in us and pave the way to eternal life.

Sanctification goes even deeper than contradiction of wrong habit or evil conduct. It strikes not only at our customs and our ideals, but it goes to the seat of wrong affections. It demands death to every wrong affection and to every wrong inner feeling and calls for the absorption of the will in the divine will. This is a glorious

demand, but a costly one and therefore it is unpopular. Sanctification calls for the death not
only to sinful acts, but sinful desires, sinful appetites and sinful affections. It goes to the
center of the human character to destroy the
works of the devil. Here is the great battle-
ground of human hearts and human lives. If
we are to die to sin, if we are to die to all that
is displeasing to God and the heart is to be made
pure and the whole life is to be submitted to
Him, it is necessary for us to do the thing that
is unpopular, something that has always been
unpopular and will always be.

Some of the opposition to sanctification is
due to the unpopularity of this truth. In spite
of ourselves we are governed more or less by the
influence others have upon us. If we hear a person or thing talked about and opposed, it is quite
easy for us to become influenced by those unkind remarks until we are prejudiced against a
man or a truth. There was an intelligent young
woman standing in a service during an altar call.
The writer approached her, seeing that she was
thoughtful and seemingly interested. She was
asked if she were a Christian. Immediately she
replied that she was. Then she was asked if she
had ever been sanctified. "No," was the quick
reply. "Do you wish to be?" and again she re-

plied she did not. Her answer was rather sudden and unexpected and was very positive. "Young lady, I can tell you why you do not want this blessing," I said to her. "All right," she replied. "If you can tell me I will admit the truth." I told her the reason was that she had been turned against the doctrine of sanctification by the unkind remarks of friends and that she had become unduly prejudiced against it. "True," she said. "Everything I have ever heard about it has been against it. I have heard it ridiculed and laughed at and thus I am prejudiced against the very word itself." "Then," said I, "if you had been so prejudiced against justification, do you think you would ever have sought and obtained that blessing?" "No," came the quick reply, "I think not." This tells the whole story of the case. People have rejected a sacred and blessed Bible truth because it has not been popular with their friends. Public opinion has oftentimes had too much influence in our choice and in the forming and fixing of our testimony. It has had more to do with us all than we are willing to admit possibly.

Misunderstanding, lack of information, unwise statements on the part of so-called leaders, the demands that sanctification makes upon men and the unkind remarks, the unpopularity of this truth among our associates have given birth to much opposition to this sacred Bible truth.

But these are not the only reasons for opposition to sanctification. We must look beyond the facts we have been considering, therefore we wish to study in the following chapter some of the grounds of the objections to sanctification we find in the minds and hearts of people.

CHAPTER THREE

Grounds of Objections to Sanctification Examined Further

In the last analysis the opposition to sanctification that deserves consideration is based upon the seeming failures, the abnormalities, the shortcomings of those who profess this high state of grace. Real opposition worthy of notice could not be based upon the Scriptures, for the Bible teaches sanctification in its entirety. The opposition could not be based upon logic, nor upon philosophy, for there is nothing more logical to be presented to the mind of man than the wonderful teachings of the Word of God concerning the fall of man, the regeneration, the sanctification, and the glorious hope that lies beyond the grave. No philosophy has ever been studied that is more fascinating than the philosophy of salvation. The logic is undeniable, and the results to the mind and character glorious. The opposition to sanctification, therefore, must be found in the witnesses to this experience.

It should not be necessary for us to deny the shortcomings, the abnormalities, and even the lapses occasionally found in the lives and spirits of the defenders and advocates of Bible holiness.

We have all seen them, though they are not found in all who profess this blessing. To deny that the quality of spirit and standard of ethics as found in the hearts and lives of some people do hinder the cause of holiness and even drive away from this pearl of great price many who otherwise might seek and receive the blessing would be useless and even cowardly. We do not wish to write an apology nor are we willing to admit that all professors of holiness break down; but we are willing to admit, and that freely, that we see failures and mistakes in many who claim this blessing—failures and mistakes that are hurtful and could not be defended either on the grounds of good common sense or the teachings of God's Word.

To what is this situation due? We would not want to apologize for that which we cannot defend, nor do we wish to condemn in wholesale fashion without a fair, impartial and unprejudiced hearing of the evidences in the case. We are therefore asking the reader, with an open mind and an open heart to look at the facts involved in the case.

First, The apparent failures and abnormalities in some people may be due to the fact that they never had the blessing of a pure heart. Perhaps they came to the mourner's bench, dili-

gently sought, earnestly prayed, but were inter-
fered with by some unwise and untactful altar
worker. They were not given time to pray nor
to exercise faith in God, but they were urged by
some human logic, or some other appeal to step
out on "dry faith" and believe. This they did
at the urge of the instructor but received nothing
except disappointment and injury. These earnest and sincere seekers after holiness are often
mistreated and permanently damaged by the
hurtful methods of untrained workers in their
efforts to instruct and help. The workers mean
well, but the injury is done, nevertheless. This
is the sad part.

These people thus misled get up and go away
with an unsatisfied heart, and feel embarrassed
to admit that they do not have what they had
publicly testified to having received. They have
claimed a blessing they did not receive and they
continue to profess it without being able to show
or manifest the essence of the grace they are
supposed to have. They break down before the
eyes of the critic or the sincere seeker after
truth, bring discredit to themselves, harm to the
cause they represent, and, worst of all, grief to
the heart of God. These people ofttimes doubt
in their own hearts that they have the blessing
of holiness, but they have professed it and they

hate to be humiliated before the people by admitting that they are wrong; and perhaps they fear that they might grieve God and dishonor Him by admitting to themselves that they have doubted in their hearts. Thus the doctrine of holiness is hurt in the eyes of the public because some people break down in the spirit and ethics, never having possessed the blessing.

Second. The seeming failures in some may be due to the fact that they have lost the experience they sought and actually found. Through carelessness, indifference, or failure to walk in divine light, or by some act of actual disobedience, they have lost the experience but still profess it. Not having it, their lives can not fully measure up to the expectations of the critic or of those who earnestly and sincerely look for fruit in them. In both cases mentioned, the failures or lapses are due to carnality in the heart. The first person never received the experience, the second had it but lost it. Both fail, for no one can manifest the spirit of holiness under all conditions who does not have the blessing in his heart. The old man shows himself sooner or later, if he is actually alive. The carnal mind may be held down but it will inject its influence into the quality of one's spirit under severe tests and provocations. The writer's belief is that it is utterly impossible in the final analysis for any man with carnality in his heart to show a Christian spirit under the trying conditions and circumstances that sometimes come to us.

Third. The failure we see in others may be due to hypocrisy on the part of some professor of holiness. This, however, would be an exceptional case in the honest opinion of the writer. There are some hypocrites, no doubt; but there are very few in the holiness circles. The great rank and file of people who believe in and profess the blessing of perfect love are at least sincere and conscientious in their effort to emulate the example of Jesus and to walk in all the light they have. It is certainly fair and just to give every man credit at least for trying to do right when he is visibly putting forth an effort to be a Christian and to live a sanctified life. It is certainly safe to assume that the hypocrites are in a very, very small minority. It is seldom the case that men who do not desire the heart to be right and to serve God would be hypocritical in an atmosphere created by the preaching of the gospel of full salvation. There may be some, we admit, but certainly this would not account for the seeming failures often seen.

Fourth. The failures or abnormalities in the lives of some professors of holiness may be due in some cases to prejudice in the hearts of those doing the examining. What we see in others depends largely upon the condition of our own mind and heart. There must be qualification and a proper background for one to see clearly and justly. In a true sense, one must be himself an artist in order to fully appreciate the work of an artist. A picture may be a masterpiece, the climax of a life time of service on the part of a world-famed artist, yet looked upon by a person who has had no development of mind and heart for the appreciation of art, will appear only as a cheap piece of canvas and paint daubed about promiscuously. To such a person the picture holds no beauty, no sentiment, no emotion, no inspiration, but to one trained and developed to see and interpret the wonders of art, the picture will present untold value. The canvas must possess the elements of art, and the person examining it must have the faculties of interpretation and appreciation. Taste for art and the ability to enjoy it are both essentials for a fair and just evaluation of art and for unbiased criticism of the artist.

In New York a few years ago in the public school system a large number of boys and girls were segregated as dull and subnormal. This was done by the authorities in order to give them special teachers and special instruction, and also in order to give the brighter children an opportunity to advance without the handicap of duller pupils to retard the program of the classes. In the meantime a prominent physician of the city interested himself in these unfortunate little ones. He made a careful survey of the entire group and examined each one with care. He soon discovered that many of the children were handicapped by faulty vision. Some were farsighted in one eye and nearsighted in the other. Some saw numbers on the board as they were and some saw them upside down. The physician fitted glasses upon these little defectives. One little boy enthusiastically leaped to his feet exclaiming, "I see it! I see it!" He had heretofore seen things in their wrong setting. Correction of faulty vision enabled him to see things as they really were. The minds of these children were all right. They had faulty vision. With glasses they could see clearly and reach right mental conclusions.

A woman sat in the home of a friend. The two women were freely discussing a neighbor who lived next door. One woman said to her visiting friend: "Look at my neighbor, if you will, hanging out clothes on the line in her backyard. Look at the spots and the dirty streaks in the clothes. That is an example of this woman, both as to her character and her conduct. I have no use for her. She is certainly an undesirable character." The visitor walked to the window and lifted it and then looked out at the clothes upon the line and saw that they were perfectly white. They were spotless. There were no streaks in them. The difficulty was that they were looking through dirty windows. Thus many people may be unable to see the beauty in the lives of others because they themselves have prejudiced hearts, unfair minds, and perverted vision.

It is utterly impossible for a prejudiced mind or heart to see truth in its proper perspective. The writer has seen people who could not get blessed under the ministry of a preacher whom they did not personally admire. They would sit quiet as death during his sermon, but when some-one was in the pulpit whom these people particularly admired they would get blessed very easily and would shout the preacher on with great enthusiasm. How strange it is that truth does not look the same when presented to us by those whom we like and those against whom we may hold a grudge or have some prejudice. It is not easy, we admit, to be fair and just in our estimate of others.

There are two reasons why human judgment is rarely ever correct. One is that if we like a person we will in all probability give him credit for being more than he is; and, if we do not particularly like him, we will underestimate his value and misjudge him.

Thus the mistakes and blunders and abnormalities we see in many people who profess sanctification may be due, *first,* to the fact that some sought the blessing and never received it; *second,* that some received it but lost it; *third,* that some few might be insincere and hypocritical; *fourth,* it may be due to the fact that the critic himself is often unfair in his mental attitude and investigation of those who profess this state of grace.

CHAPTER FOUR

THE EXPERIENCE OF HOLINESS AND THE ETHICS OF HOLINESS DIFFERENTIATED

There is a vast difference between the experience of holiness and the ethics of holiness. To fail to distinguish this difference makes it impossible to reach a fair conclusion regarding the doctrine of full salvation. Especially is this true if we are to take into account the witnessing and testimonies of people. If we were to settle the case purely on the statements of the Bible and the definition of scholarly men, the matter might be different; but the fact is, we cannot disregard human testimony and human life. The people in general do not read the Bible very much; and what they know about the Word of God they pick up here and there through sermons and quotations in various ways. The most of the study that is done regarding religion and the Bible comes from an investigation of the lives of people who profess religion. It becomes necessary, therefore, not only to study the Bible and Christian doctrine as set forth by the people and scholarly teachers throughout the centuries;

it also is necessary to give consideration to the lives, to the testimonies, and to the ethics of people who present themselves to us as Christians. We are forced therefore to study both the experience of holiness and the ethics of holiness; the one being taught by the Bible and the other being presented by human witnesses.

First, let us notice the experience of holiness. The experience of holiness is the work of God in the human heart, wrought by the Holy Ghost in answer to a living faith. Since the experience of holiness is God's work, it must be perfect. God is without fault and without failure at any time. What He does is done perfectly. No defects have ever been found, nor can ever be found in the work of His hands. His work is not only perfect in quality but in extent as well. The quality of His work and the degree of His work are beyond improvement. All that divine wisdom plans to do for man, in and through the work of divine grace, is fully accomplished. It is perfect and complete. Let no man criticize what God has done.

It is not uncommon to hear people remark that when they were converted they received what they termed, "the real thing." To be sure they did; and so did everyone else that was ever converted. God does not give to one person a better case of religion than He does to another. He is fair and impartial in His dealings with all human beings. He has no pets nor favorites. He loves all alike, and His work is the same in all cases. It is true that some people may have a better background for training and preparation for conversion. The results to the world in conversion of one man may be greater than another. One person may make greater use of his religion than another does; but the work of God is the same in one man as it is in another. In regeneration, all receive forgiveness of sins, new life coming into a dead soul, and they are cleansed from acquired pollution. Every person that was ever converted received these blessings or obtained these results.

The same is true of sanctification. God does a perfect work and a complete work for everyone. It sounds like spiritual pride to hear one remark that when he was sanctified he got "the real thing." The implication is, whether intentional or not, that some receive a very light case, one hardly worthy of consideration or continued possession, while others are greatly blessed of God and receive something so colossal that they are above ordinary people and have something that they can not lose. This is a wrong and erroneous attitude in the matter. Sanctification is

sanctification. Nothing more and nothing less.
God is the Sanctifier of the human soul. Those
who receive the blessing stand in glorious relationship to the Lord so that He is not ashamed
to call them brethren. He is not ashamed of
any of them. They are all His brethren and
they dwell together in the unity of spirit and
oneness of heart and of purpose. They have all
received pure hearts and have been perfected in
love so that they can love God with their whole
spirit, mind, soul and body.

It is readily admitted that some people pass
through what may be termed a cataclysmic state
which is more marked by emotionalism than
others. In some there is more struggle, more
pungent conviction, more effort in seeking God,
so far as outward appearances are concerned,
and after the struggle is over there may be
greater demonstrations of belief and more mani-
festations of emotions, but this fact is no proof
that God gave to one a greater blessing than He
did to another. It is no evidence that one received a better case of regeneration or sanctification than did another. Some of the most
demonstrative people, are the quickest to give
up and deny the faith. Some of the quietest and
most unassuming souls are the most faithful;
yea, faithful unto death. Some people seem to

have more fire than others, more power than others, if we are to judge fire and power by emotionalism and outward demonstrations, but this would be an unfair test. The thing that counts in the last analysis is faithfulness to Christ, Christlikeness, and quality of spirit. The struggle in getting sanctified is not a determining factor in the extent or quality of the work done in the soul. Some people have a harder time to get the consent of their own minds to yield perfectly to the will and purposes of God than others do, but in the last analysis, the conditions that bring the blessings from God to the human soul are a perfect yielding of the will, and living faith in Christ.

The work of God is perfect in every case: whether we shout or keep quiet, whether we laugh or weep, whether we walk or sit down. Demonstration is desirable if done in the Holy Spirit; that is a matter with the individual and the Lord. But the outward demonstration or the quietness of the individual are not determining factors in the quality of the work done by the Holy Ghost in the heart. When God sanctifies a soul He cleanses the heart from all sin, destroys the old man, kills out sinful self and worldly ambitions, and fills the soul with love to God and man, against which there is no law.

The work of sanctification is pre-eminently a divine work. We are not sanctified by growth or suffering or death or the fires of purgatory. It is not evolution. It is a divine accomplishment wrought in the human heart by divine power. Paul says that the very God of peace is to sanctify us wholly. This reflects the glory back on God where it should be. The praise can not go to man or to any process or achievement of his. It must ultimately rest on the Giver of each good and perfect gift, the God of our salvation, the Savior of the world.

The work of God in sanctification is not only a divine work, and perfect, but it is also perfectly satisfactory to him in whom and for whom the work is accomplished. It may not satisfy others, but it always satisfies him who receives the blessing, the blessing that is of God complete and perfect. The thousands of people that may be found throughout the earth who have come into possession of this pearl of great price will testify with one accord that they were not disappointed in the gift received from God. Such unanimity of testimony could not be found concerning the satisfaction that results from any human glory or the indulgence of appetites and passion in the pleasure of sin. But a testimony to the sanctifying blessing received from God through the baptism with the Holy Ghost and fire, in the sanctification of the human soul attests the perfect satisfaction of the human heart, in and through this blessing. One of the outstanding proofs that one has been sanctified is that he is perfectly satisfied. No man is so contented as the one filled with the Holy Ghost and fire; as the one with a pure heart filled with the love of God. Satisfaction is safety. No man is safe until satisfied. The woman who is not happy with her husband is never a strong woman. In such case she is open to temptations, and allurements, and inducements unknown to the woman who is perfectly satisfied with her married life. Satisfaction means strength, and sanctification always brings perfect satisfaction. Thus a man sanctified wholly is not only a satisfied man, but a strong man to meet the temptations, the battles and the offers of a sinful world that seeks to induce him to leave God.

The question is often asked, "How can we hold the young people?" That answer is simple. It can be done in only one way, namely, to get them filled with the Holy Ghost so that their hearts will be perfectly satisfied. We take the position that any young man or young woman can be so completely satisfied by the presence of

God, by the Bridegroom of the soul, that the inducements and the temptations and the allurements of this world can have little influence over the mind, the heart or the life. The church can not meet the competition of the world by resorting to the same things the world uses to keep its devotees in submission to sin and its pleasures. The church can not hope to win by bringing into her own life the movie, the dance, the pool hall, the billiard room. She must meet the competition of the world solely on the ground of the fulness of the Holy Spirit satisfying the human heart so that one is so contented and satisfied that he does not have to resort to the world's garbage cans for food.

One proof that we are sanctified is that we are satisfied. All unsanctified people are unsatisfied. They may not be dissatisfied, but they are unsatisfied. This leads one to think sincerely that the people who run after tongues and other strange demonstrations, forgetting that purity and divine personality are the great assets of the soul, have never been sanctified; or, if so, they have lost the blessing. Sanctification satisfies the soul. It is the work of God, perfect and satisfactory. There is no fault to be found with it by the person who receives it. It may be criticized by others, but never by the possessor of this pearl of great price. And, after all, the testimony to be given credence is the testimony of the man who receives the blessing, not the one who criticizes or looks on, who has never tasted to see that the Lord is good in the bestowment of this great gift.

Thus we would assert once more for emphasis that holiness is God's work. It is complete; it is without fault; it is perfect; and it is satisfactory to him who receives it.

The ethics of holiness is man's work and therefore imperfect, if not always so, at least to some extent.

Conduct is based upon two things, namely, knowledge and conscience. Some teachers of psychology would prefer to say that conduct is based upon conscience alone, and then attribute to conscience two faculties. *First,* impulse, which is accepting or rejecting right or wrong when it appears; *second,* discrimination, which is the faculty of conscience that tells right from wrong. In this short discussion we prefer to hold that conduct is based upon two things, knowledge or light, and conscience, and then confine conscience to one function, namely, impulse, accepting or rejecting when right or wrong appear. In any case we will all admit that some people have more knowledge or light than others have, and that some consciences, with proper training and education, have greater power of discrimination than others. These facts must be taken into consideration in the study of ethics.

People are not equally well informed. Some have greater light than others, some have keener powers of discrimination. This fact must be again and again emphasized. Quality and quantity of light or knowledge will have a bearing upon what we do, and our ability to distinguish between right and wrong, will determine the nature of our conduct. It is difficult to imagine how our ethics can rise higher than our knowledge. Imperfect knowledge will likely result in an imperfect system or code of ethics. This is obvious. God commands us to walk in the light; that is, to do the best we know, and live up to the extent of our information. We are to bring up the "bottom of our lives to the top of our light." The higher the light, the greater distance the bottom will have to come if the two are to meet. No man can live beneath his light and stand justified before God and the bar of his own conscience. But he must not be too readily condemned if he is doing the best he knows. But this is no excuse for us to hide behind. We should not only strive to walk in the light we have, but we should endeavor to become better and better informed each day. We should grow in the knowledge of the Lord Jesus Christ. It is not enough to walk in the light we possess, but moral responsibility enforces upon us the necessity of striving for additional light, energetically and conscientiously. Thus, knowledge is a factor in any code of ethics.

Concerning knowledge, there are two facts that must be kept in mind continuously. *First,* that it is enjoined upon us by the Word of God to walk in all the light we have in order to be justified before the Bible, before the conscience, and before God. Second, it is obviously our duty to seek light, to increase in knowledge each day in order that we might approach nearer and nearer toward the standard of perfect ethics. At the present moment lack of knowledge might be an excuse for faulty ethics, but if the power lies within us, and the opportunity is presented to us to increase our stock of knowledge, and acquire more light in order that we might take from our ethics the faults and shortcomings, we are then forced to put forth every effort possible to measure up to this tremendous responsibility. We must walk in the light we possess and continually seek additional light and raise the standard of our ethics.

Conscience, the other factor in ethics, or that function of conscience that we call impulse, can be perfect and must be perfect. The power to discriminate may be imperfect, but impulse must be perfect. No man can rightly claim any degree of grace in his heart who does not accept right willingly and gladly when it is presented to him and he perceives it as right. No man can claim the possession of religion who knows the wrong and yet hesitates to take sides against it. Conscience must say "Yes" to right and "No" to wrong. There is no middle ground and no time for argument. The soul that hesitates at this point immediately enters the fogs and haze of doubt and disobedience, and loses his bearing and also his favor with God. When right is perceived it must be immediately accepted and defended with determination; and when wrong is perceived, it must be immediately rejected, condemned, and opposed.

The sanctified man in reality faces but one vital question, namely, What is the will of God for me? To always know the will of God is not an easy matter, but to do the will of God when once it is known is the outstanding duty and joy of every consecrated soul. Many of us have spent sleepless nights and feverish days trying to decide what the will of God is concerning many of the details of our lives; but it is difficult to imagine how any conscientious child of God could weep and struggle to get the consent of his own mind to do the will of God when once he knows the divine plan and purpose for him.

It is evident that we can have a perfect conscience if conscience is to be defined purely as impulse, but if discrimination is to be attributed to conscience, then conscience is not perfect and not likely will it ever be. In this case its perfection would depend upon its education.

Our difficulty lies in the fact that conduct or ethics is based not only on impulse, which is accepting right and rejecting wrong when it appears, but it is based upon discrimination, or knowledge, as well. Knowledge may be imperfect and naturally is, therefore our ethics may show imperfections, which fact accounts for much we see in people that we deplore.

Our powers of discrimination are often at fault. One person shows greater discrimination than another. For example, some claim that it is positively wrong to drink coffee or to eat hog meat, others think it is perfectly all right. If one perceives wrong in either, if his conscience raises an objection, then he must not partake of what he considers wrong. He must follow his conscience and his information or knowledge.

Now let us grant that the man who sees harm in drinking coffee or in eating hog meat has greater light than another, that he has greater discrimination. In that case he must follow this impulse and the light he has. If the other person sees no harm in it his conscience will not be affected by it. Some think men can get to heaven and eat hog meat; in fact, they think the more he eats the sooner he is likely to get there, for the chances are that too much of it will shorten one's life, at least in many cases.

Thus it is evident that though the heart is perfect toward God and the work of God in the soul is perfect, the experience of holiness within us is without fault, our ethics may not be perfect because of limited light and lack of keen discrimination. There are people who would die for the right, and suffer the loss of their lives in opposing wrong, who at the same time might be dull to distinguish in matters of proper and acceptable ethics.

Fortunately for us all, God does not demand that we have perfect minds. Such demand would necessitate two things in order to justify such divine requirements. *First*, If God demands that we all have perfect minds, He would be compelled because of His justice, to permit us to be equally well born. *Second*, He would have to give each an equal chance to develop and improve the mind with which he is born.

But neither is the case, as we all know. People are not equally well born. A child of a healthy father and mother will have a better chance physically than one born of sickly parents. The same is true of the mind. The child of well and strong parents will have a better chance in life in the nature of things than one born of a father and mother with weak and dissipated brains. Again, not all have the same opportunities to develop the minds they have. Some are secluded in some out of the way place without educational advantages, without even proper home training. What can be expected of them? Is God to exact the same requirements of them as He exacts of those who have been born in the very lap of opportunity and have had good home training and every educational advantage? No one can think so and feel that God is kind and just. Since we are not equally well born and since we do not have equal opportunities, God can not demand the same mental standard of us and at the same time be just. But God is just toward all, and therefore we can safely assert that He can not, and does not demand perfection of us from a physical and mental standpoint.

It is evident that we are not mentally perfect, that God does not demand that we have perfect knowledge, that our powers of discrimination are not faultless, and consequently it is well nigh impossible to produce a system of faultless ethics. It is hard for one's conduct to rise higher than his knowledge. Our powers of impulse, accepting right when it is apparent and rejecting wrong when it is evident, are perfect and must ever be perfect; but again we emphasize that the difficulty arises in the realm of discrimination. Lack of perfect minds and imperfect knowledge account for many faults in the ethics of sanctified people; and, in fact, of all persons who profess to be Christians.

Our estimate and judgment of others are often wrong from the fact that we fail to distinguish between the experience of religion and the ethics of religion. We will not and can not present to the gaze of critics a faultless system in the ethics of life and conduct without background of perfect knowledge and discrimination. This fact every fair-minded man and woman must accept.

Furthermore, we are free to assert that anyone looking upon the conduct of others with the thought of examining or judging, in the sense that God permits us to examine and judge (we know the tree by its fruits), should be fair enough to assume that he himself might have bad judgment, imperfect vision, or faulty powers of discrimination. The element of charity, therefore, should be in the heart of the critic as he knows his own limitations in seeing correctly and in reaching wise decisions and also in his ability to render unbiased and impartial verdicts.

The position we have taken in this discussion is not an apology for mistakes in Christian people, nor is it to be understood as an effort to justify those who lack knowledge or comprehension and discrimination. Lack of knowledge and light should never be taken as an excuse for shortcomings and defects in our ethics, but should be looked upon with contempt and tears and every effort should be put forth to remedy our defects that we might not mar the beauty of Christian life and bring injury and discredit upon the cause of God. Once more let us assert that it is necessary to discriminate between the experience of holiness which is the work of God in the human heart and perfect and satisfactory, and the ethics of holiness which is man's work and therefore usually imperfect. Let God be praised and honored for the work He does in the hearts of men and if there is fault to be found in the followers of Jesus Christ let the blame for such fault lie at their door and let not God be charged with folly for He is not to blame. He purifies the human heart and fills it with His own personality, and satisfies every longing of the human breast. But men are so limited in their powers of discrimination that they do not always exhibit before the eyes of the critic or the conscientious seeker for truth that code of ethics for which men look and have a right to look.

CHAPTER FIVE

THE FOUNDATION OF RIGHT ETHICS

The ethics of holiness must have a foundation. This consists of two things, namely, inner divine purity and what the Bible terms light. Ethics should be the product outwardly of a state that exists inwardly. Ethics should be an exposition of a right condition of character in which purity and knowledge are mighty and indispensable factors.

The basis of ethics is being—being that is essentially right, righteous, being with unity of character of Godlikeness. Perfect character would produce perfect ethics. The more nearly perfect therefore, character is, the higher will be the standard of ethics produced. Thus thought should be given always to the condition of one's character in the effort to raise the ethics of one's life.

Knowledge is an essential. Knowledge knows, sees and understands conditions and situations and can even analyze them from top to bottom. But knowledge, while clear and transparent and necessary, is not sufficient. Wisdom also is an essential. It is greater than knowledge because it sees relationships and adjusts things to harmony. It not only sees problems but finds a solution for them. It not only sees beings but relates them rightly and properly. Knowledge, it has been said, deals more distinctly with the clear, cold intellect, while wisdom enters the moral realm, and it is in the moral realm that ethics is planned and wrought out. Knowledge can see things but wisdom must relate them and adjust them to harmony and co-operation.

Holiness, too, is an essential. Holiness must furnish the motive for action and conduct. It is not enough to see things and relate them but it is necessary to put into our actions a worthy incentive. Holiness of character removes the selfish elements that would distort, sidetrack and misuse energies to some wrong or useless end. It is apparent that no man can ever hope to raise his ethics in the final analysis higher than the state of his character, especially as related to holiness of heart. This is basic. This is fundamental.

Love is another essential. Right relations can never be established and maintained without the passion of love—love going out toward those toward whom our actions are directed. Love is a power, not passive but active, seeking, going out, unselfishly sacrificing for the good of others.

To live rightly, to fulfill our divinely appointed destiny, we must have unity of character in Godlikeness, with knowledge of right, with wisdom that will properly relate things, with holiness of heart that will furnish a proper motive for all actions, and a mighty love passion that will unselfishly seek the good and happiness of others.

Paul commands the Christian to work out his own salvation with fear and trembling. This does not mean what some have unwisely interpreted, namely, that we are merely to work with our hands, to toil and to sacrifice and deny ourselves for others in order that we might be saved. It does not mean that we are to merit heaven by good works. Service has its place in Christian life and Christian conduct. This fact is undeniable; but we can not work our way into a state of grace nor into divine favor nor into heaven. The rich young ruler seems to have had this misconception. Running to the Master he asked, "What good thing shall I do that I may have eternal life?" With him it was something to do. He felt that there was some great achievement that he could work in his own life—that he could perform some service or make some sacrifice that would bring him into divine favor and into possession of eternal life. There are many followers of this man in the world. Many a poor broken-hearted man suffering spiritually has gone with sincerity of purpose to ministers of the gospel or other advisors for help, and instead of being prayed for and urged to exercise faith in God, he has been told to redouble his energies in church activity, to render more service in some great social program. Social service is good, and service will help any one by reflex action; but service is the product of life rather than the originator and creator of life. We do because we are. Primarily our state of soul determines our conduct. Life is the cause of conduct and not the result of it.

Outward service and inner divine life should be considered as effect and cause. Service is the effect and inner life the cause. God in the soul produces our outward life, but right living outwardly will not work salvation into the heart of man.

Salvation must be worked in before it can be worked out. Life is an inner creation. An oak truly can not be produced until God has worked into the acorn the germ of life which is potentially a tree. Soil, sunshine and rain may work it out, but a great divine Creator must work the life into the heart of the acorn before that life can be crystallized, or presented in some outward form.

Involution must always precede evolution. One can not evolve a hundred dollars out of the bank until he has involved a hundred dollars into the bank. Taking money out of the bank is comparatively easy. The difficulty is in placing it on deposit. It is a simple matter to evolve the funds after they have been involved. It would be very difficult for a public speaker to evolve a message out of his brain and heart before he had worked one in through study and mental toil.

We cannot work in a state of holiness; but God can work a state of holiness into us, and then we can work it out in our daily conduct. The following illustrations might serve to make clear the truth under consideration, namely, working out our own salvation with fear and trembling.

An artist stood before a canvas with paint and brush. He looked upon that blank canvas and smiled complacently as he exclaimed, "What a picture! What a masterpiece! What a work of art! What sublime beauty!" "I see no picture," said his friend who stood near him. "I see only a piece of canvas without line or curve." The artist turned and said, "Come back in a few years and you shall see what I now look upon with deep feeling and emotion." Time passed, the artist with care and effort worked conscientiously, touching the canvas here and there and measuring distances, combining colors, and transferring from his own mind to the canvas the work of art. His task was finally accomplished. His friend returned and when he stood before that picture after twenty years of absence, he exclaimed, "I see it! I see it now!" and then with emotion he said, "I can understand why you smiled with satisfaction twenty years ago over the beauty you beheld upon that canvas. Where," asked the friend, "was the picture when you first smiled?" "It was in my mind. In my soul," replied the artist. "What you see was first worked into my own inner being and with years of toil and effort I have worked it out and placed it upon the canvas that others might see what I saw in the beginning."

Another man stood before a crude, rough piece of marble. He, too, evidently was moved with joy. He saw something sublime. With chisel and mallet he worked untiringly for many years. Here a little and there a little he cut away the material, freeing from its imprisonment the beautiful form of an angel. When the chiseling was all done he laid down the mallet and the chisel and polished the figure, even going over it with his fingers to give it the last and most tender touch. Then he stood and felt that sense of peace and joy that comes to the soul after the achievement of a great and worthy task. His friends stood and admired and praised both the artist and his work. Where had this angel been? From where did it come? Out of the crude marble? In the final analysis, No. It had come from the soul of the sculptor. He had worked out of his own being the angel that stood before the gaze of an admiring world. It was first an inner creation and then an outer accomplishment. He had worked it out.

A builder stood on the street corner with his arms folded. He saw before him a vacant lot with raw materials, brick, lumber, sand and cement, laid about seemingly promiscuously. But what did he really see? He looked upon a building, a finished product. He looked beyond the vacant lot, beyond the rough, crude material heaped upon the ground. He saw a structure that would do honor to the most skillful builder. The house was within his soul. It was an ideal, it was an air-castle. It took him weeks and months of hard work and ceaseless toil to place that material into form that represented the finished product. It was something within him. Something spiritual, something mental, that he had put into concrete form in visible aspect for the good of mankind.

A few years ago the writer was in a certain city where a picture was being shown, "The Man of Galilee." Crowds were going to see it. Interest was keen. He joined the crowds in viewing this work of art. The picture was so arranged that one could look upon it with a light shining upon its face so as to bring out the most striking effect. The people stood before that picture in silence with bowed heads. They were distinctly awed. No one seemed to be willing to speak: all were too absorbed in that work of art before them. Looking upon the picture the writer could see in the distance the little mountains of that land of promise that had been the silent witness to so many sacred scenes and tragedies. Nearer was the lake that looked so restful, quiet, and undisturbed by wind or storm. Still closer, only a short distance was the Man of Galilee kneeling with His head lying on His arm that rested upon a shelf of rock. He had been praying through the still watches of the night. Alone. Alone. Bearing the burdens of all mankind upon His sacred shoulders, His passionate heart bursting with pity, love, and compassion. The veins in the side of His face were visible and His entire form indicated suffering.

He was so real, so lifelike, that one felt that he could walk into His presence and kneel by His side and ask permission to help Him bear the burdens and carry the load that was so obviously upon His tender soul. As people walked away they were visibly moved with the deepest emotion and stirred with the spirit of devotion and worship.

"Oh," said I, "if I were an artist and could paint a picture of my Lord that could move the multitudes, and make Christ more real to this lost world, what would I give?" Then it occurred to me that I am an artist, an artist of higher type than he who uses the brush and the paint. An artist of more importance than the man that stands before the crude marble with a chisel and mallet. An artist of more significance than the one that stands upon the platform with violin and bow; an artist of more significance than the great singer who moves the emotions of men with quality of voice and depth of feeling. I am an artist called upon to paint the picture of Jesus Christ upon the canvas of everyday life, a picture of Christ that man can see and admire, a picture that will cause them to think more of religion, have more respect for the Bible, a picture that will create within them a hunger for righteousness and a passion for Christ's likeness, a picture that will lift Christ up before the world that man may see Him and be drawn to His great side, a picture that one can see and be constrained to glorify the Father who is in Heaven.

After crossing the continent from East to West for many years, one day I determined to turn aside to see the Grand Canon of Arizona. I had looked upon many of the great wonders of this land and of Canada, but when I stood upon the brink of the Grand Canon and for the first time looked into its depth and saw its width and length and its resplendent beauty and glory, I was filled with feelings of admiration and ecstasy such as I had never had before. I stood there looking into a canon one mile deep, fourteen miles wide and two hundred miles long, with the waters of the Colorado winding like a silver thread down through the heart of the great canon, appearing and disappearing as they made their way toward the southern lands. What a wonderful day it must have been when God plowed out the Grand Canon of the Colorado.

As I stood there I thought of a picture that I had enjoyed as presented by the pen of John Stoddard. He tells of an artist who had married a beautiful young woman who herself was an artist. The two had gone to the Grand Canon on their honeymoon. The young artist walked with his bride to the edge of the canon before daylight. There he blindfolded his bride and standing by her side waited until the rising of the sun. When the sun had come up and filled the canon with light so that one could see the great cathedrals, pictures of battleships, Chinese walls, or any other of the great wonders of the world the imagination might present to one's mind, he removed the blindfold from the eyes of his bride. When she looked for the first time upon the glory of the Grand Canon she dropped to her knees, sobbing, and told her husband that should he ever attempt to paint the picture of that glorious scene she would be tempted to divorce him, that it was too sacred, too sublime for an artist even to attempt to reproduce.

Late one afternoon I noticed a Japanese artist with brush at hand and paints before him, trying to paint the picture of the canon and of its glorious beauty. Crowds gathered around him. Seemingly he paid no attention to them. Here and there he touched the canvas with his brush, seemingly oblivious to everything around him. Occasionally the wind would blow leaves and dust in the air, but he continued touching, changing, shading that picture to make it as nearly as possible like the canon into which he looked.

At first I was tempted to say it was a shame and disgrace to paint a picture of the grand sight that lay out before me. Different ones watching the artist paint made remarks, some favorable and some unfavorable. As the shadows thickened and the sun sank behind the mountains the artist began to bring out with wonderful skill the form, the color that drew from the lips of everyone expressions of admiration.

Watching the artist and looking upon the Grand Canon I said to myself, "How could a man ever see anything so sublime and consent ever afterwards to say an ugly thing or think a little thought or to have an unkindly feeling toward one's fellow men." I stood in the presence of glory, of beauty, of sublimity.

Turning away from the Grand Canon I said to myself, "I would like to be an artist that could paint that picture as I saw it," but the passion of my soul is to paint a picture of Jesus Christ, a living Savior, an example to a dying world, that others might see Him in all of His beauty and of His glory. Mountains may be sublime and Grand Canons glorious, but personality exceeds them all, and divine personality, the personality of Jesus Christ, is the greatest of all great things to be looked upon by the human eye and enjoyed by the human heart. To be an artist, a real artist, a true artist, an artist that can paint the picture of Christ on the canvas of life, that should be the ambition and passion of every child of God.

At once the responsibility so heavy and yet so sacred came down upon my heart with such weight it seemed too much to be borne. It occurred to me then that man is called upon to enter the realm of art more sacred than that of paint and brush, more sacred than that of marble or of music; that I am such an artist, and that I fall so far short in presenting before the eyes of man the ideal, the inner creation within me, I felt my heart would break.

It is much easier and simpler for God to work a perfect ideal in the human heart than it is for a poor human being to paint an acceptable picture of that ideal in his outward life and conduct. Christ is within us the hope of glory and without fault. We can see Him within us as He is, perfect and glorious, and this inner divine image stirs us to joy and holy ecstasy. But lack of knowledge and lack of experience and lack of genius and skill, these cause us to paint poorly that glorious picture within us. We make the line upon the canvas too light or too heavy.

Nervousness causes us to press the brush with too much emphasis. We are tired and worn out. We mar the picture. We make a mistake, we are sorry and weep over it. We did not mean to do it but the damage is done nevertheless. The picture is injured. The world looking upon us is disappointed.

It is some consolation to us all that God looketh upon the heart and not upon the outward appearances. It is a comfort to know that God looks upon the acts of one's life in the light of the motive that prompts that act. But even this does not and can not satisfy the conscientious child of God. The true servant of the Lord not only wants to reach heaven, but he desires to carry the largest possible number of souls with him on the journey. He desires to make the Bible, the blood, the personality of Jesus Christ as attractive as he is able to do. To make all manner of excuses for weaknesses, to apologize for faulty ethics without tears of regret and passion for improvement is cowardly and contemptible. It should be the passion of every child of God not only to have a good experience of salvation, but his very soul should crave that genius and ability to reproduce the experience in the ethics of his life that he feels and sees so distinctly within him.

Indifference is little less than sinful and criminal. It is cheap to boast over a good experience and pass the criticisms of others concerning one's shortcomings and defects with a sarcastic glance or a smile of ridicule, and boast that we do not care what others think of us or whether they like us or not. This is foolish in the extreme and beneath the dignity of a high-class man or woman, leaving out of consideration altogether the fact that one is a member of the highest aristocracy on earth—the family of prophets and priests and apostles and saints of all ages of whom the world is not worthy.

Christian people have done themselves more harm than all the critics outside the ranks of God's people combined. Holiness as a doctrine could never be refuted from the standpoint of the Bible and of logic and beauty of fellowship, but from the standpoint of imperfect ethics we are bound to admit with sadness of heart that many things occur that bring humiliation to those who believe the doctrine of full salvation.

The question, What constitutes a sanctified man? might be asked and answered with profit. It is a perfectly legitimate question and while it involves much, can be and should be answered frankly and definitely. Much depends of course upon how much is to be included in the definition. The following, however, would seem sufficient. A sanctified man is a man—just a man, not an angel, but a man—a man with all of his appetites and passions that are legitimate and normal. These powers are necessarily God-given and natural to the human race. These are not only divinely bestowed, but are to be kept as an essential part of human nature and human life. God gave them for a purpose, and if they had never been degraded by sin and prostituted to unnatural and abnormal uses they would have been held as sacred and useful. A sanctified man therefore is a man, just a man; not an angel, but a man with all of his appetites and passions that are normal and legitimate; a man that is consecrated to God body, soul, and spirit; a man whose heart has been cleansed from all sin and filled with the love of God so that he is enabled by the circumcision of the heart to love God with all of his soul powers, and his neighbor as himself. He is a man who possesses the appetites, the passions, the physical and mental powers with which God originally made him; who has consecrated all to God and His service; whose consecration has been accepted, his heart purified, and filled with divine love and possessed by divine personality. He now stands a consecrated man, cleansed from all sin and filled with God and is able to fulfill the law of love in his attitude both toward God and man. Against such there is no law, nor could there be a just objection to such state on the part of any man.

Who could reasonably object to a scriptural consecration of oneself to God and to His cause? Is it not the duty of every church member, of every child of God to lay himself in perfect submission at the feet of the Lord? Should every one not be able to say from the depth of his heart, "Thy will be done"? Is it not the duty of every Christian to permit his own will to be swallowed up in the will of God? Is there anything abnormal about a man's being perfectly consecrated to God? This is beyond question the duty of every man, and is a reasonable service. It is not far fetched nor abnormal, but the right, the legitimate, and the normal attitude for every child of God to take. He should be dead to sin and to the world and seek only the glory of God and the promotion of His kingdom in the earth, and subordinate every other interest of his life into conformity with this purpose and ideal. His citizenship and affections are in heaven while he lives upon the earth.

Again, What is abnormal with the cleansing of the heart? Do not all men need heart purity? Is this not a proper, a reasonable and scriptural standard? What is there about a pure heart to be objectionable? Should our motives not be pure? should our affections not be right? should the heart not be free from all sin and worldly contaminations and worldly affections? There could be presented no just cause for objection to heart purity. To this fact all agree.

Again, what should be wrong with a Spirit-filled heart and life? Should not all men be negatively delivered from sin, from sinful affections, and then be positively filled with the Holy Ghost? We must be enabled to love God with a whole heart and even to love our enemies. This standard can not be reached without a pure heart and the indwelling of divine love and divine personality.

A sanctified man is a consecrated man, a purified man, a man filled with the divine love so that he can fulfill the law of love. What an idea! What a standard! What a passion should stir the soul of every man to pray and seek to reach that standard where he can know beyond a doubt that he is consecrated completely, that his cleansing is thorough, and that his love is perfected. This is God's standard as taught by the Bible, and is within the reach of every earnest, conscientious, willing soul.

The foundation of right ethics is a right condition of being. Ethics should be the outgrowth or product of an inner state of normal rectitude and uprightness. Inner consecration, inner purity, the presence of divine personality within a heart filled with the love of God must constitute the background of that standard of ethics God presents to mankind as an ideal for him to strive to reach in this present life. No one could scripturally deny the power of God to make the heart right; no one would argue that Christ is unable to fill the soul with His own love. These facts being admitted, we assert that man should endeavor to make his outward life conform in every particular to that glorious inner life and inner power divinely bestowed.

This places a tremendous responsibility upon every child of God. In the chapter following we wish to present briefly the value of right ethics.

CHAPTER SIX

THE IMPORTANCE OF RIGHT ETHICS

The importance of right ethics can not be overestimated, for it determines our relationship to people as holiness determines our relationship to God. If the experience of holiness is not acceptable to God, we can not be perfectly related to Him. God could not be satisfied with any of His children to the fullest extent that have sin or sinful affections in their hearts. He could not be contented to look upon His children with qualities of heart that would be unlike Christ.

If the ethics of holiness is right, we can be properly related to our fellow men. The condition of our heart determines the attitude of God towards us and the standard of our ethics will determine the attitude of people toward us. No man who loves the Lord can be satisfied merely with getting to heaven. If that is the only meaning the Christian life has, the most of us are certainly mistaken in our conception of moral obligation. God gives us to understand that we can not have holiness toward God without peace toward man. Thus the importance of right relationship with humanity is clearly indicated. We are to follow peace with all men in order to have holiness without which no man shall see the Lord. No man can be right with God and yet intentionally wrong with his fellow man. In spite of our wishes the effects of our ethics upon the lives of others will have much to do with their attitude toward religion and Jesus Christ, the world's Savior.

The method of presenting Jesus Christ will determine the influence Christ has in the world. It will also determine the extent of our own influence over the lives of others. Our ethics will draw men nearer to us and to Christ and increase our influence for good over them, or it will drive them from us and tend to discourage them in seeking Bible salvation. If we want to do good, if we want to be a blessing, we must seek to make our ethics commensurate with that glorious state of divine purity and divine beauty within us.

"When I am lifted up," said Christ, "I will draw all men unto me." This expression constitutes the very heart of ethics and influence. We are to lift up Christ for He is to save the world, and not we ourselves. Poor ethics will tend to draw the attention of the world to us, good ethics will tend to center the attention of men upon Jesus Christ himself.

Two women go to the meat market on the same day. They both purchase meat from the same cut. One prepares and serves her meat in an attractive manner so as to arouse the appetite and nourish the body. The other woman is a poor cook and serves her meat on a dirty table, an unattractive plate, and with surroundings that tend to dry up the gastric juices and discourage the guests. In spite of all argument it must be admitted that the manner in which food is served on the table has much to do with the acceptability of it and the good it accomplishes. Food well served tastes better than food that is poorly served. A dirty knife and fork, an unclean table cloth and unattractive surroundings will have an effect upon the appetite. With everything clean, attractive, and wholesome one can enjoy his food much more and get far more benefit from it. It is a wise woman who tries to make her service at the table most attractive and presents the food in the most attractive way possible. It is not enough merely to serve food; it must be properly served.

The same is true of religion as expressed to others through the ethics of our lives. Two men can come upon the platform to preach the gospel. Both may love the Lord and both may carry a passion for lost souls and both may have a great message; but the manner in which they present the truth to the public will have great bearing with the hearers. If one man is uncouth, rough, boorish, untutored in his mannerisms, awkward in his gestures, and faulty in his language, he is likely to attract the attention of the people to himself and cause them to forget the beauty and value of the message he is presenting. But the man that can present the truth of Jesus Christ without any particular abnormalities or strange mannerisms so that the people hear the truth and see the picture of Christ without looking upon the speaker himself will naturally accomplish greater good. The value of our ethics is seen in the fact that it will make Christ more acceptable or less acceptable.

When is a man or woman well-dressed? This is a question which is not easily answered. Perhaps the dress question is one of the most perplexing that has ever confronted the Church of Jesus Christ. What is proper and what is improper? We understand it is easier to tell people what they may not wear than it is to tell them what they may wear. It is the opinion of the writer that a man or a woman is well-dressed when it is scarcely noticeable how he is dressed. Dress that brings out the beauty and attractiveness of the person himself rather than the pe-

Dress question /

culiarities of the dress is normal. Personality should constitute the attraction rather than the garments one wears. Men are well dressed when one does not notice how they are dressed. The same is true of women. Food is well-served when one is not attracted to the way it is served but the thought and attention are rather centered upon the food itself. Ethics is right when it so presents Jesus Christ as to cause the people to see Him rather than the man or the woman presenting Christ. We are to let our light shine and our good works appear that men may glorify our Father who is in Heaven. We are not the attraction; Christ is the attraction. The dish or the plate does not feed the hungry. It is the food upon the plate. The need of the world is not fine clothes, but fine men and women wearing clothes. But the plate and the clothes have an effect. The world can not be saved by ethics; but the ethics of a Christian's life will make Christ appear beautiful, or unattractive.

Again, the value of ethics is seen not only in the fact that it brings out the beauty of Jesus Christ and His attractiveness, but there is also a reflex blessing upon the character of the man or woman who talks and acts as a Christian should. A wrong impulse that crystalizes in conduct becomes stronger, and if that wrong im-

pulse continues to be yielded to and continues to
crystalize in deeds, it will finally become over-
mastering. On the other hand, if to a right impulse, expression is given and if it is allowed to
crystalize in conduct, it will become stronger and
stronger and the inner state of a man will become more and more acceptable. In this sense
the condition of the heart produces ethics, and
in a reflex manner ethics also has something to
do with the forming of the character. Good
ethics therefore will not only cause the human to
keep in the background and push Christ to the
front, but it will also strengthen and increase
those powers that promote one in the battle for
Christ's likeness.

Since good ethics is important it should be
the desire of every conscientious man or woman
to raise the standard of his ethics in every possible way. It has been stated already that the
divine image can be worked within us immediately; but the working out of our salvation is to
be with fear and trembling, a constant and daily
exercise. No builder will become perfect in the
execution of his art without careful and conscientious practice. A man does not have the power
to take sin out of his heart or to put Christ
within his heart. That is the work of God himself. But man does have the power by exercise

to improve his building day by day. The ideal within us is to be worked out slowly with pain and care. After we are saved and sanctified and sin is removed from the heart we are conscious that our faculties have been twisted and warped by wrong habits, and it takes time to bring those powers back into proper relationship. This calls for improvement, correction and conscientious effort on our part. We have wrongly expected young converts, or people sanctified only a few days, to reach the standard of ethics in word and deed that one would produce who had been on the road to heaven forty or fifty years. This is unreasonable. If the young convert is expected to present such a high standard, then the person that has been serving God for so many years would certainly be condemned if his standard should not be higher than the one just leaving the world and entering the kingdom of God.

There is room for improvement in us all. Not room perhaps for improvement in our experiences in the forgiveness of our sins or the cleansing of our hearts. God has forgiven us fully; He has cleansed the heart and filled it with His love. He would not be able perhaps to improve the quality of the meat nor the quality of the cloth that we bought at the store, but we can improve in our method of serving the meat or making the garment from the cloth. We have power to improve in our method of executing our art before the eyes of men. There is not only room for improvement, but we have the power to improve. *True!* And if a man does not improve in the standard of his ethics day by day he is not doing his duty before God and man and could not be justified before the bar of his own conscience. Let us note some ways to improve our ethics.

First. We should realize that the ideal within the heart is far superior to the methods we have employed in executing that ideal. Without this realization one would not advance very fast. One must realize that he can improve and *(1)* that he should improve. If one has the false notion that he is doing just as well as he could do, he will certainly not put forth much effort to raise his standards.

Second. We must know that the power lies within us to improve our ethics. We are told *(2)* educationally that there are two great problems that every boy and girl faces in college. One is the problem of horizon. Education is supposed to enlarge the horizon of one's life; his vision should be pushed out to include greater space and take in greater sweeps of territory. The second problem he faces is the problem of mastery. He must be made to understand that he is not to become a slave, but a master. He is not to be subjected to the environment and influences of life around him, but he is to stand a victor and a conqueror over everything that would hinder his progress and mar the beauty and dignity of his manhood. He must realize that God has given him a power to change his surroundings to his own liking. This is the glory of man. He is not the slave of his environment, but the master of it. This same realization must come to every child of God. He must know that the Holy Ghost within him working out through him can change the environment about him, making him an overcomer, or will enable him to adjust himself to conditions. Standards are to be determined and a desperate struggle put forth to reach them within and without.

Third. One can improve his ethics by reading the Bible. His Word is a lamp to our feet and a light to our pathway, and day by day it should shine brighter and brighter. The Bible is our chart and compass. It is the book that tells us how to live and what to do. Life has two great problems and only two, and the Bible is the only book that can help us to solve those two problems. The first one is what to do. Men must do something; men will do something. One of the great principles of moral obligation is doing something. What must I do? That is one of life's two fundamental problems. The second one is how to do it. What must I do and how must I do it? These two problems sum up life in its entirety. The Bible answers these questions as no other book can. It tells us what our duty to ourselves is, what our duty to our fellow man is, and what constitutes our duty to God. Then the Bible tells us how to perform the duties and obligations we are under. It tells us how to talk, how to treat our neighbor, how to live in peace with our fellow man, how to be courteous unto all men, that we are to love our enemies, to do good to them that persecute and despitefully use us. The man who lives the best life is the man who reads the Bible most and who reads it conscientiously for direction in the molding of his character and the shaping of his ethics.

Fourth. We should pray earnestly every day. It is the opinion of the writer that no man will be able to live the kind of life the Bible and his own conscience demand of him unless he prays daily for strength and wisdom and for guidance. The church has suffered more through a neglect of prayer than any other one thing in the world's history. Worldliness will wreck a church, but worldliness would never be possible in a church if the people prayed. Worldliness in dress, and worldly habits, are not the cause of backsliding; they are the result, and prayer is the only thing that can keep the spirit of the world out of the church and enable church people to live simple, devout, and exemplary lives.

Fifth. We must carry a passionate love for others. The careless word, the unkind deed, the unethical expression are usually the result of coolness of heart and indifference of soul toward others. Nothing can assure the home of peace, harmony, understanding, and happiness like love. The more love one has in his heart, the less likely he is to speak the quick or the harsh word. The greater the amount of divine love in the soul the less danger there is in wrong conduct or discourtesy toward others. Of all the needs of the world, the greatest is love: more love in the heart of man for his friends and his enemies. If I were called upon to give in one expression the cure for ethics that injure the cause of Jesus Christ and brings trouble between neighbors I would say the solution is in one thing—a passionate love in the heart for mankind.

Sixth. We should have a spirit of Christian courtesy toward all men. It should be the resolution and the fixed purpose of every heart to treat with kindness and courtesy every person with whom he comes in contact. Lack of courtesy on the part of Christians toward one another is an outstanding paradox; it is beyond comprehension. How one church member can talk about another, how one preacher can find fault and express that fault about another preacher is beyond belief.

Men should so live that they can have respect for themselves, for a house divided against itself can not stand. If one's conscience and affections are warring against each other, weakness is bound to follow. If mind and heart do not agree, progress becomes very difficult if not impossible. If a man be in harmony with himself it is probable that he will be kind and courteous toward his immediate family. There should be the greatest degree of Christian courtesy between husband and wife, father and son, between mother and daughter, and brother and sister. The home itself should be an example of beautiful courtesy between the members of the family.

Again, we should seek to be courteous toward one another in the church. We need more warmth, more cordiality, more friendship in the assembling of the people of God in the house of worship. There is a social touch, a human touch, a touch of friendship that cheers and encourages that should not be overlooked in the house of

God. The rich should mingle with the poor, the educated with the illiterate. There should be Christian courtesy at all times in every department of the church. The preacher should treat with respect the most humble and the most ignorant members of his congregation and should listen with respect and courtesy to every suggestion from such a one, and the members of the church should realize that the preacher is the anointed prophet of God, the shepherd the Lord has placed over the people, and God's anointed should be treated with dignity and respect. Criticism should be unknown, and unkind statements should be avoided with the same care that we would avoid murder or adultery. The tongue should be kept in control, and every expression by word, deed, or attitude should be kind, for God has commanded us to be courteous unto all men.

Finally, the Christian should be courteous toward the unsaved, toward the most wicked man in the community, even toward his bitterest and most deadly enemy. A peaceful answer often turns away wrath, and if kindness and courtesy will not win in life's battles, harsh and oppressive methods certainly will not win. Love never faileth, courtesy never faileth, for real courtesy, genuine, unadulterated courtesy, is a natural and spontaneous expression of love. May God fill the church of Jesus Christ with divine love and then enable us to realize the importance of a right standard of ethics. And may He give us a desire not only to realize the importance of right ethics, but a determination to strive to find better and more effective ways of expression for the glorious, divine life within us.

CHAPTER SEVEN

Religious Experience and Religious Education

There are two schools of religion, both of which are supposed to be orthodox. These two schools occupy extremes. It has always been the case, and doubtless will ever be true, that the tendency of individuals and of religious movements is to swing to some extreme. First, there is that school of religion that emphasizes the importance of religious education to the neglect of religious experience. Those in this school of religion do not overestimate the importance of religious training, instruction or education, but they underestimate the value of Christian experience. There are those that emphasize the importance of experience to the neglect of training and education. These do not overestimate the importance of experience but they seemingly forget the value of religious training. It is not difficult to locate these two schools of religion, for they are to be seen every day by even a casual observer. Some churches place all emphasis on the training side of religion and others place the entire emphasis on the experience. One believes that training is everything and the other seems to hold that experience is the only thing of importance. One naturally studies the outer life to the neglect of the inner, and the other studies the inner life to the neglect of the outer. One is inclined to deal only with processes and the other only with crises. They are both right and yet both wrong. If the two could be combined wisely and properly we would have a system that would stand uncondemned before the Bible and the wise conclusions of our own mind.

In the first class mentioned you will naturally find the cold and unspiritual churches or people —those that may still hold to forms of doctrine and put their emphasis on a social program, but the matter of personal salvation is almost entirely overlooked by them. Children are urged to attend Sunday school, to study the Bible, and attend to all functions of the church program. The matter of a change of heart is forgotten. Regeneration is no longer urged, and the thought of being filled with the Holy Ghost is foreign to them. They may have a Decision Day when all of the children old enough are asked to decide for Christ and come into the full church membership. There is no seeking for a change of heart, and no one is asked to pray for the witness of the Spirit; in fact, there is no prayer connected with decision. It is a matter of the mental assent, a matter of accepting Jesus Christ with the mind, with no thought of the fruit of the Spirit to follow in the life. They are urged to be loyal to the church, to live respectable lives, to do right, to be ladies and gentlemen, to be ethically correct.

An organization of this kind may contribute to the social and ecclesiastical life of the world. It teaches good citizenship, loyalty and devotion to an organization, and its members are likely to get the idea that the organization of which they are members is the greatest and most worthy institution in the world.

This school of religion teaches a system of high ethics that is commendable and of much value, but the tendency is away from the blood, sacrifice, the penitent tear, sorrow for sin, passion for lost souls, and deep devotion to Christ in the inner life. Like the church of Ephesus, they have good works, commendable labor, and take sides against all forms of immorality, have faith in their system of belief and organization and patiently toil for its promotion; and they may do what they consider to be right (and many do this for His name's sake); but they have lost the first love, if they ever possessed it.

With them religion is more of a form of godliness, but without the power thereof. This school of religionists faces the following imminent dangers:

First. They are likely to substitute works for faith in Jesus Christ for personal salvation. They do religion, and the expression most common among them is, "I am trying to treat all men right." They believe in water baptism, church membership, and fidelity to the ordinances of the church; and the final hope of salvation and eternal life lies in their good intentions, in their good works, and their clean living. With such people, religion is a matter of works, conduct and ethics. Christ as a person is largely forgotten, and works have been made to take His place.

Second. The second danger that faces this school of religion is the substitution of a system for a Person. We should all recognize that there can be no Christianity without Christ; that there can be no salvation without a Savior; that there can be no fellowship without a person. The world has always tried to accept the results of Christ's work in the earth without accepting Christ himself. This tendency is becoming more and more noticeable in religious circles. The old familiar doctrine of infidelity is being advanced from the pulpit, namely, that Christ is a good man, that His teachings are wonderful, but that He is a Savior only in that He is to redeem the world by the power of a right example. We are told to take His word, His teachings, His example, without particularly accepting His divine personality. To such people He is only a dead Christ, and lives only in the memory of men and women as a great historic character, and His immortality is purely impersonal. This is the natural tendency of the school of religion that forgets Christian experience in its teachings. Its converts declare allegiance to the Church and its teachings and social programs rather than allegiance to a personal Christ who is more glorious than all organizations and systems of belief on earth.

Suppose I take the teachings of Christ as my own standards and try to live outwardly by them, and do not accept Christ himself in my heart. To be sure, the results will make my present life more acceptable ethically, and of more value to the world, but this attitude on my part will not remove my load of sin nor will it pass me into that state of happiness which the soul longs to enjoy beyond the grave. We must have a crucified Christ as well as an ethical Christ. The world needs a living Christ more than it needs a dead Christ. His personality is of more value than His teachings or His example. We need Him, and without Him we must all perish. A standard is necessary, but without an inner power to reach it the standard would prove ultimately of no avail. Humanity is so corrupted by sin it can not lift itself into a state of righteousness nor into salvation. The power of sin must be broken in the human heart by the spirit of God that worketh within us.

Third. Another danger that faces this school of religion is the substitution of reformation for transformation. The difference between the two is obvious. Reformation deals with the outer life and transformation deals with the inner life. A reformer always begins his work at the circumference and proceeds toward the center, while the transformer begins at the center and works out toward the circumference. An organization of men, one that is purely human, will always work at the outer edge of life, for that is the only place it can work. Jesus Christ has a different method, and always starts His work in the heart and makes it right first. He goes beyond the ethics, beyond the appearances, to the affections, the desires, the passions, the will, the conscience, with His quickening power and transforming grace, endeavoring to harmonize the inner life of man with His own Godlikeness. Thus two results are accomplished at once. The heart is changed, and the life is turned in the direction of godliness and heaven.

The world needs education, to be sure, but it needs transformation far more. If we make the heart right the life will be adjusted accordingly, at least to the full extent of one's knowledge and light. But the mind might be enlightened without a guarantee of a right life. It does not always follow that men do what they know to be right; but it is true that they usually do what they want to do. Not all enlightened people are good, not all ignorant people are bad. Knowledge of right is of great value, but the love of right is far better and more dependable.

Religious training will have a tendency to make people do right; it will cause them to see the law of cause and effect, the law of sowing and reaping, the value of right living in results to health and long life. But no degree of training, culture, and refinement can change the affections of men and determine their attitude toward sin and its pleasures. God can so fix a man by His transforming power as to cause him to hate what he once loved and love what he once hated. Such a result is not human, it is divine. It does not lie within the power of psychology or philosophy to change the affections and desires of men. So far as sin and righteousness are concerned this can be done only by the divine Spirit working a miracle within man's character.

Every child should be taught the truth, for we are saved by the truth and not by error. The entire human race should be taught the very best principles known to man; and the standards of right living and right ideals should be kept ever before the mind and heart of society. But no standard of religious education, as valuable as it may be, can ever take the place of the transforming power of the Holy Spirit within the human heart. It is not difficult to find people who are trying to serve the cause of righteousness with their hands, while their hearts and desires crave the world. This is not God's wish nor God's standard. We must not only serve the interests of truth and righteousness, but we must delight ourselves in the law of the Lord, and the heart must enter fully and freely into every effort to serve Jesus Christ and do good in the world.

Fourth. The fourth danger to which we call the reader's attention is that of a gradual lowering of religious standards. All will acknowledge that we are influenced by our environment, and ultimately we absorb—at least, to some extent we imbibe—the spirit of our surroundings, and finally we are in danger of accepting the decisions of people among whom we live in matters of conduct. If the problem is left to training and education the tendency will be to lower the standards rather than to raise them, so far as the spirit and the conduct of the world are concerned. In conferences and public gatherings it is common to hear the cry raised that laws against dancing and card playing should be repealed because they have become ineffective in some of these older organizations. The argument is advanced that such laws cannot be enforced, and the argument is correct to this extent, namely, that no church can live on good rules, or even sound doctrine, alone. The only way to save a church and make it effective is to keep it spiritual. It must be filled with the Holy Ghost. Right belief is a necessary foundation, but insufficient. Honesty will not save a man, nor will orthodox belief. We must have the divine spirit within our heart working the image of Christ within us. There must be an inner power, an inner life, a quickened spirit that will hold us in the old paths. The tendency of humanity is to take the way of least resistance. Nobody enjoys opposition. Persecution is something we do not seek or enjoy. Our natural tendency is to avoid it wherever possible. It is practically impossible for the Church to maintain high standards of religion and of ethics unless such church keeps the regenerating power of God's spirit and seeks to be baptized and remain filled with the Holy Ghost and fire. Good resolutions, good intentions, legislation, and legalism will finally break down unless there is a living spirit within us to propel and drive us up and on like the steam in the locomotive. The Holy Ghost himself must furnish such power and energy within the heart of the believer.

Another danger faced by that school of religion which lays all emphasis on religious education, is the forming of a human religion with no God in it. Essays will take the place of the Bible. Historic characters, other than those pictured in the Bible, will be preached instead of the prophets and the apostles. Hell will be laughed at, and immortality doubted. The resurrection will be passed with unconcern, and a belief in a life beyond the grave discarded.

This is a dark picture. How terrible it will be to face death with no personal Christ to stand by the bedside and comfort the passing soul! At such time it would be futile to ask for water baptism, church membership, clean morals, devotion and faithfulness to a system or organization, to comfort or sustain one when the death rattle is in the throat, and the sweat of death stands upon the brow, and the bells of eternity ring in the ears; when one feels the mists of death falling in his face and realizes that this world is passing and eternity approaching, he needs a living personal Christ on whose bosom to lean, and in whose heart to find comfort and solace. We can thank God for a personal Christ. We can know Him as we know an earthly friend. It was the comfort of Paul to rest in the strength of such a Christ, and every other child of God has the privilege that Paul had. Who doubts the tendency of this age to eliminate God and everything divine from its system of belief? Who can not see that science is being substituted for divinity? Who can not see that the conceit of the human heart is clamoring to put God off the scene of action, claiming that man has the power within himself to save himself? Who has not heard it said that it is a humiliation to admit that we are fallen, and that we must have a force outside of ourselves to lift us into higher realms? This is the tendency of the present day, namely, to substitute a human religion for God and Christ and the Holy Ghost.

Can man save himself? Can man reach that standard of manhood which Christ lifted up, and yet not have the Christ within him? Is man not fallen? and does he not need a Savior? Is he not utterly undone? Has he not failed in all countries where Christ has not been accepted? Has not civilization itself perished of its own weight and defects where Christ has not been? With all the preaching on the brotherhood of man and the golden rule, does not man fail when swept by some passion of hatred and prejudice? Was the World War not an evidence that the polish on the surface of civilization is insufficient? Is it not a fact that humanity, though galvanized outwardly, perishes within without that health-giving spirit to touch life at its very center? We are bold to repeat again that churches are in danger of substituting human religion, social service, and a human program for prayer and heartfelt religion and a personal Christ.

Fifth. Another danger of this school of religion is that it will finally lose its ministry and its young people. Men are called to preach, not merely because of an atmosphere of learning and of education, but rather in a revival spirit. From the old-time Holy Ghost revival there will be young men called to the ministry and to the mission fields. If a church stands and sees its preachers die off at the top and younger men are not entering at the bottom, it is easy to prophesy the final outcome of such movement or organization. Men must enter the ministry with a burden for souls, and not for an occupation or a profession. If money or honor were the motive back of the ministry the world would be able to win promising young men to its own ranks in competition with the Church, for in the final analysis the world can offer more money and greater honors to young men than the Church is able to do. The only hope of the ministry is a Spirit-filled atmosphere that creates unselfishness, self-denial, and a burning passion for lost souls. This is the atmosphere that gives birth to preachers and missionaries.

How shall we conserve the life of our youth? This cannot be done by competition with the world. The world can get pay for its programs and the Church must offer hers free. The world can enter her programs wholeheartedly, and the Church must enter hers with more or less misgivings and divisions of opinion, if her methods are to be similar to those of the world. This very fact means defeat. The Church and the world are two separate and distinct institutions. They can never mix in the sense that the Church goes with the world to the same sources for pleasure and enjoyment. A spiritual atmosphere is a romantic one, and anything romantic appeals to youth.

It is a great mistake to imagine that deep spirituality will not appeal to young life. Singing with feeling, music, joy and enthusiasm, all appeal to the young, and these are characteristics of a deeper spiritual atmosphere and will satisfy the youth of the land as nothing else can. In this atmosphere young people will soon see that every legitimate and normal craving of the body, of the mind, and of the spirit can be perfectly satisfied within the kingdom of God. It is our contention that the outstanding inducement of Christianity is that it offers every good thing that man could ever need and enjoy, and that it eliminates every evil influence and power that would hinder and destroy. The salvation of Jesus Christ saves us from everything wrong and to everything good.

A church that loses its passion for souls will ultimately lose its ministry and its youth. The preacher must have soul passion. He must enter the ministry, not for what he can get out of it, but for what he can put into it. He must enlist in the ranks of God's servants with a feeling and a conviction so deep-seated and so immovable that his very salvation depends upon his obeying God in preaching the word. He will get that spirit not from training—he must get it from God. The church that depends upon a manmade plan or a manmade ministry, or competition with the world upon the platform that the world offers, must finally perish so far as God and salvation are concerned. A church that does not offer to its young people a peace of soul, a rest of heart, a fulness of the inner life that brings results greater than the world can offer, must perish.

In conclusion, we might summarize the dangers faced by that school of religion which emphasizes religious education to the utter neglect of religious experience. First, there is danger of substituting works for faith; second, the danger of substituting a system for a person; third, the danger of substituting reformation for transformation; fourth, the danger of gradually lowering its religious standards; fifth, the danger of having a human religion with no God in it; and sixth, that it will finally lose its ministry and its young people, in that the ministry will die off at the top and the young men will cease to enlist in its ranks, and it will lose its young people in that they will go to the world for their pleasures and satisfaction, thus mixing the church and the world so that you cannot tell the one from the other.

The other school of religion is the one that emphasizes religious experience to the neglect of religious education. It does not emphasize religious experience too much, but it emphasizes religious education too little. In this list we will find the holiness churches in the main. Those that dwell a great deal upon regeneration, the new birth, the witness of the Spirit, eradication of carnality, the fulness of the Holy Ghost, Spirit-filled life, and kindred doctrines that have much to say about the Spirit and His work in the human heart and upon human character.

No doubt the reader has looked upon camp-meetings and other revivals held throughout the length and breadth of the country, where the altar was crowded day after day with earnest seekers for salvation, and saw clearly that no provision was made to care for the products of these meetings. There was no place these tender lambs could be fed. They were forced to return among the wolves where they would be devoured before the next campmeeting to be held a year hence. They had no soul food, no encouragement, and very little inducement to press on in the battle for God except the help they received directly from the Lord himself. Those means of grace such as the prayermeeting, the ministry of the Word, encouragement in

Christ's likeness, were denied them. They went on Sunday to hear a minister that would abuse them and criticize their experiences and find fault with the doctrines that led them into great peace of soul. The time came when it was obviously necessary to create an atmosphere of encouragement and hope for people that believed in and experienced the blessing of full salvation. Thus for a goodly number of years there has been a distinct move toward crystallization into organizations that would give instruction and education as well as furnish emphasis upon initial salvation.

There is little gained by getting people converted unless they can be encouraged to faithfully follow Jesus Christ. There is little gained by getting people sanctified wholly unless they are taught how to live a sanctified life, so that they can keep the blessing and be an asset to the kingdom of Jesus Christ in the earth. Many a man has started toward heaven and given up in discouragement because he did not know how to live a Christian life. Thus the necessity of religious education.

We would profit perhaps by noticing a few dangers that face that school of religion which emphasizes experience to the neglect of religious education. We repeat that they do not overvalue experience, but they underestimate the importance of religious training.

First. They are likely to feel that their duties end at the moment they encourage a man or woman in the community to seek God in conversion or sanctification. They are likely to feel that when they pray a person through at the altar their responsibility is completed, that their duty has been duly performed, and now they can turn away to other interests with perfect satisfaction. They seem to forget that they are their brother's keeper, they forget that they owe a debt to every man to love him, to boost him, and encourage him as long as they both live. Initial salvation is important. No one can get to heaven without a change of heart. Jesus told Nicodemus that he could not enter into the kingdom of heaven unless he was born again. The writer of Hebrews tells us that without holiness no man shall see the Lord. Thus renegeration and sanctification are both essentials for heaven. But what has been gained if the regenerated man is not cared for and instructed in truth and sound doctrine so that he will persevere and go on to holiness, continuing to walk in divine light? What advantage is there in getting a man baptized with the Holy Ghost and fire if he is not instructed and taught and encouraged to keep the blessing, and to go on increasing in the knowledge of the Lord Jesus Christ and persevering in things of divine grace and usefulness? The danger is the tendency to forget the results of the altar service and to leave the persons who pray through to go out unorganized, untaught, untutored, to wander about aimlessly, and to become food for wolves.

Second. Another danger of this school is that they are likely to neglect the children; and such has been noticeable in all holiness churches and circles. Who has not attended the big campmeeting, or the big revival meetings, and noticed fathers and mothers on the front seat feasting upon the blessings from God and rejoicing in the peace of heart that they have received from the Lord, and at the same time permitting their own children to wander about the meeting, or to run aimlessly over the grounds, or to sit on the back seat laughing, tittering, disrespectful, and on their way to destruction. These parents love their children, to be sure, and they are praying for them, and many times they are under great burden, weeping day and night, and even fasting while they pray for their families; at the same time they have overlooked the value of the ethics of life, they have forgotten that our children are saved by the truth. God must have a foundation, a background, in order to work effectively for the salvation of our loved ones. These parents never go to Sunday school; perhaps they do not think it is necessary; they can love the Lord and be religious and stay at home. Their children are left to desecrate the Sabbath, to neglect the training in mind that the Sunday school would give them. They grow up without religious instruction. Note the two extremes.

There are some churches that depend entirely upon the instruction of the child and the decision day for his salvation. Then there is the church that places too little emphasis upon the Sunday school, or the religious education of the child, and depends only and solely upon the altar service for its future. Both schools are wrong. We cannot get a child into the kingdom of God by joining him to the church. Neither are we likely to build strong characters and give to the world useful lives if we stop our work when the altar service is over. Experience is good; so is religious education. They are both of great value, and without them the cause of Christ cannot prosper.

Third. The third danger of this school is neglect to develop the graces and the talents and gifts of its young people. The Lord can use a polished instrument with more effect than one that is crude and unpolished. A surgeon might open a boil with a dull, rusty jackknife and relieve one's agony, but it will be far better to have a clean sharp lancet that would enter the boil and remove the pus without so much pain and danger. There are many gifts and talents lying dormant in young men and young women of a church, that would be of incalculable value to God and humanity if properly developed. Religious training and education, and the use of such talents can bring them into their highest possibilities. We are to be blessed in order to bless others. The Sunday school, the Young People's Society, public testimony, songs, and preaching on the street corner, in the shops, in fact, service to God and mankind in general, together with training, instruction, education, will bring out those powers within us that would otherwise be lost to the world and to God. We must be saved, we must be sanctified, but we must also be trained and instructed in the things of God and in matters of service.

Thus we have called the reader's attention to the two extreme schools of religion. *First*, the school that emphasizes religious education but neglects experience; *second*, the school that emphasizes religious experience but neglects religious education. They both have strength and yet they both have weakness. They are both right in that each emphasizes an essential, they are both wrong in that each fails to emphasize an essential that it is a tragedy to overlook. Is it not strange that humanity has such a hard time keeping poise and balance? For example. We need the radicals and the conservatives. They both have a place. Without the radical element of the church we would soon become stereotyped, fossilized, cold, and formal. Without the conservative element we would become rash, harsh, uncharitable, and would plunge into extreme and unwise enterprises that would wreck the movement. We have the radicals and the conservatives. Would it not be a wonderful thing for every man and every woman to have within himself a proper proportion of the radical elements and the conservative elements? One to counterbalance the other? It is poise of character that is needed by everyone.

It is equally true that we must have the element in the church that dwells upon the necessity of having the spirit of holiness, the essence of Christ's likeness, the fulness of God's Spirit, the power, the fire within us that should characterize full salvation. We should also have an element in our ranks that believes in a proper training of the child, of young manhood, and proper education for the leaders and all members of the church. Why not be balanced and well poised in all things? If we wish to have a church that will stand the tests of all time, that will endure while the storms beat upon us, we must have a proper foundation laid, and the superstructure must be right. Without experience of heart the church would be a mere clubhouse, it would be without effectiveness in the salvation of mankind. On the other hand without religious training and religious education the church could not be an effective means of reaching the world as God wills it should be. It would be in danger of two things in particular. First, inner dissolution and disintegration of its own ranks and its own departments; and second, utter failure in its effectiveness to grip the mind and the heart of a thinking world.

Thus we plead both for religious experience and religious education, both for heart holiness and right ethics, both for the infilling of the Holy Spirit and the outward training that would make us effective in the hands of God.

CHAPTER EIGHT

CHRISTIANS—GOD'S ADVERTISERS

"Be thou an example of the believers, in
word, in conversation, in charity, in
spirit, in faith, in purity."

Every age of the world has been character-
ized by some outstanding feature. We have had
the dark ages, the age of the revival of learning,
an age of discovery, an age of exploration, an
age of colonization, a literary age, an age of
poetry, one of science, and an age of invention.
Every period of the world's history has had
some prominent characteristic that has featured
such time. It is true that no age of the world
has had one characteristic alone. Each age has
had many characteristics overlapping and inter-
locking.

This particular time in which we live is a
commercial age. We have science, philosophy,
literature, art, invention, and perhaps all characteristics of all ages to some degree; but the
predominating spirit of this time is that of commercialism. The spirit of business, of money

making, has given color to every interest of human life in this age and generation.

There are two great facts that stand out in this commercial age. One is manufacturing. Seemingly everything is being manufactured to-day that could be conceived by the mind of man. Everything from a cambric needle to a steamboat. There doubtless are things yet to be produced but it is hard to imagine anything that is not being turned out of the great manufacturing plants of the world that mankind could ever use. If a manufacturer hopes to make a success he should produce something that is needed by the people; and the more general that need the greater his chances of success. This is the secret of the manufacturer of a certain kind of automobile. He made a car that everybody needs. While perhaps few people wanted one, for a long time the necessity for such a car had been felt by the masses. Not only so, but he made an automobile that was within the reach of the masses. First, he made something that was needed; and second, something that was within the reach of the people in general. This shows the wisdom of the man and of his great organization.

The second great factor in commercialism is that of advertising, for it would be useless to manufacture goods unless such goods could be put on the market, sold, and utilized or consumed by the people. The manufacturer could not continue without a market for his product. It is just as necessary therefore to advertise as it is to manufacture. The great value in advertising lies in the fact that it creates a demand for goods. It does not create a need, but it creates a want. It arouses a desire for something that people need. A good salesman is not a man who can make the people buy what they want, but to get them to want what the salesman has to sell. This is the secret of advertising. It is to arouse a desire in the minds of the public for the manufactured article.

Millions, yea, multiplied millions of dollars, are spent annually to advertise certain commodities. "Eventually, why not now?" "There's a reason," who has not seen this statement hundreds and hundreds of times? There is a psychology in advertising that must be taken into account. The plan of the manufacturer is not to get the people to buy flour, but to get them to buy a certain brand of flour. Not to buy clothes, but to buy clothes of a certain make. The effort is put forth to influence one to call for a certain kind of soap or toothpaste instead of merely calling in general for such articles. Certain pe-

riodicals published have received as high as
$10,000 for the back cover and as much as
$5,000 for an inner cover for one issue of the
publication. It would seem impossible for great
commercial organizations to receive adequate
returns from such outlay of expenditure, but
experience proves that they do. Thus millions
are added each year to the sum total spent in
advertising the world's business.

The greatest manufacturer in the world to-
day is God Almighty. He is not making steam-
boats or automobiles. He is not making clothes
or other articles of usefulness. The Lord is in
the business of manufacturing Christians. He
announced centuries ago the coming of Christ
for the purpose of dying for the world. Christ
came and gave His life on Calvary that all might
be saved, and in that act He provisionally saved
the whole world, but He did not actually save
anybody except those without power of moral
choice. God's great task is to influence the individual to seek salvation and accept Christ.

In order to do this God must advertise His
business. Thus each Christian is an advertiser
—either a good one or a poor one—for Jesus
Christ and His great salvation.

A poor salesman in a clothing store might
try on a man every suit of clothes in his hangers

and have nothing that the purchaser would particularly desire. The salesman might then become impatient and say to the prospective purchaser some unkind and cutting word that would cause him to leave the store without buying; and, not only so, but with a resolution never to return. Another salesman is so kind and courteous and respectful to the potential buyer as to make him desire to do business with the concern. Thus the salesman becomes an asset and he makes friends for his organization. Everyone is a good salesman or a poor one. Every Christian is a good advertiser or a poor one.

When a man is converted or sanctified the Lord could take him to heaven immediately. But He does not usually do that, for He needs the influence of such person to advertise His religion in the earth.

No man enjoys being a gazing stock for others. The suit of clothes that hangs on the wax figure in the show window is there, not for its own pleasure, or its own glory, but for the honor of its owner. Thus we are to become the lights of the world, cities set on a hill that can not be hid. Not that we might appear good and great, but that we might show forth the glory of Christ and make men see the value of salvation and cause them to want it.

Christ Jesus tells us how we are to be advertisers for Him. He says, "But be thou an example of the believers."

First, in word. Words stand for ideas, they have meaning. It would seem that Paul in this statement had in mind more especially the fact of truth. He seemed to emphasize that we should have the truth, that we should be orthodox, and that our word should stand for ideas, ideals and meaning that would form a sort of foundation for Christian character and Christian life. Doubtless he meant also that we should watch our words that they should be not only positive and meaningful, but that they should be void of hurtfulness and injury to others. He exhorted Christians to advertise Jesus Christ by the word of truth, the word of soberness, the word of life. Negatively the word should carry no evil, and positively it should convey truth, comfort, and life.

Second, he exhorts us to be an example of the believer, or an advertiser for Christ, by our conversation. Conversation, as we all know, is a final revelation of the quality of one's inner character. No man should be judged by the single word, incident, or act of his life, but rather by the trend of his life. It has been said that two things always reveal character. One is mood. A man will reveal himself in his moody moments as he will perhaps at no other time. The second way to test character is to watch a person under great pressure. The moments of weakness represent the final strength of a life. No man is stronger than he is in his weakest moments and in his weakest spots. Conversation is the straw that will indicate the way the wind blows. Out of the fulness of the heart the mouth speaketh. If the heart loves the world conversation will soon reveal that fact. If the heart loves money the conversation will run more or less along the lines of money and business. If the heart is lustful and unclean the conversation will indicate such fact by the dirty or the semi-smutty joke and talk that would indicate that the mind dwells on unclean objects. If a man will talk, and talk very long, particularly under pressure, or in his moody moments, his conversation will soon reveal the contents of his heart. Paul tells us to have Christ enthroned within us, the hope of glory; and if this is accomplished the conversation should indicate that Christ is within us, and should advertise the Bible, the church, and Jesus Christ, the world's Savior.

One might wonder if his conversation, in the shop, in the factory, in the bank, in the store, in public or in private, would lead his friends and associates to believe him a Christian. The best method of advertising Christ is not to bore and harangue, and ridicule and coerce, but it is rather that unconscious influence which comes from a spontaneous, a natural flow of conversation out of a clean heart full of God's love.

Third. We are to advertise Christ by our charity. Be thou an example of the believer in charity. This has to do with our patience toward others and our relationship with them.

The world's troubles all come from one source, namely, conflict between personalities. The blowout of an automobile tire, the loss of a little money, a reverse in business, a rainstorm is not trouble. These constitute an inconvenience, but real trouble comes from that conflict between persons where there is disagreement, hard feelings, and broken fellowship. For example, if a man and his wife have a disagreement and can not get along, that constitutes real trouble. A conflict between the human will and the will of God is trouble, real trouble, a source of great sorrow.

All real happiness also comes from one source and only one. Namely a right, legitimate, and proper relationship between personalities. Fellowship with God is the greatest source of human happiness known. When the will says yes to the divine will, and man is reconciled to God, he enters into that relationship of peace and happiness and fellowship that makes life glorious. There is nothing that can be compared with it. This is a pleasure and a happiness the sinner misses. He is not to be condemned nor abused, but rather to be pitied because of the great loss that he ignorantly suffers. Fellowship with one another constitutes real happiness; when such fellowship is based upon community of character, such character being in harmony with God, His will, and His nature. If the happiness of life consists in right relationships with God and with one another, then think what we miss when we permit little differences to rob the heart of a great source of pleasure that is rightly ours.

We would all confess readily that our greatest difficulty in life consists in putting up with other people. Our chief troubles are not with things, but with persons; and our tendency in human relationships is to be uncharitable and unyielding. The Christian's standard is charity toward all and prejudice toward none. Are there hypocrites, we should not see them. Are there people around us that get on our nerves? We should not allow them to do so, for when a man gets on one's nerves he is only one step from his religion.

good quote

The writer reluctantly admits having been in his early life grieved at God on two counts. First, I remember times when I preached, seemingly without the help of the Holy Spirit, and such occasions are certainly sad and unpleasant memories. I recall upon one occasion having preached in human strength only. There seemed to be no unction and no spirit in the meeting. On the way home I asked the pastor how he liked the message and he replied, "All right." I told him that I wanted the entire credit and all of the glory, because I preached the sermon myself. Seemingly God had nothing to do with it. I went home that night and lay on the bed with breaking heart, and wept the most of the night, and begged God to relieve me of the ministry, for I felt that I was a failure. But before daylight the Lord seemed to impress me through His compassionate love and infinite patience that I must try it again. The next night there was a great victory. God swept down upon the people with power and the altar was filled with seekers and happy finders. Going home that night I told the pastor that if he liked the message he could give God the credit, for the Lord had preached that night while I had done the preaching the night before. The reader can easily imagine that there was a great difference between the two. I was distinctly grieved at the Lord because He did not seem to help me on some occasions. While praying over this matter the Lord made it very clear to my heart that He had done far more to reach those people than I was doing, and I asked God to forgive me and I have never been grieved at Him about that since.

The second thing over which I permitted myself to be hurt at the Lord was the fact that I made up my mind that certain people didn't have any religion, and yet the first meeting I was in with them they were blessed of God, and I felt the Lord was blessing people that didn't have religion. Who has not been guilty of that same offense?

In praying over this matter I told the Lord there were some people I had put up with as long as I could, and the Lord asked me if it had ever occurred to me how much He had put up with in me. Immediately I asked Him to change the conversation. That situation had not occurred to me before. Since then I have been more charitable with other people, feeling that if God could put up with me I should be charitable toward others. Oh, for more charity, for more longsuffering, for more kindness and more forbearance. The average man is having a great struggle and he needs sympathy and compassion

rather than criticism and fault-finding. Jesus
Christ wants us to win others by advertising His
grace in the human heart, that enables us to
have charity for others.

Fourth. We are to be examples of the believers in spirit. The king preferred Daniel above
all the princes because he had within him a right
spirit. This is the quality of soul that causes us
to estimate the value of people. One woman
said to me once—and she is a very gifted and
prominent woman—that if she were going to get
married again she would not choose a man because he had money, as desirable as that might
be. Nor would she select a man because of
brains, though she admitted that she would not
object to his having a few brains. "But," said
she, "I would choose him for his temperament."
And I replied, "In other words, you would
choose him for the quality of his spirit." "That
is correct," she said. "If I am to live with a man
through life I want one with an agreeable and
pleasant spirit." Who would deny the wisdom
of this woman's conclusions in such a matter?
The men that live longest in the affections of
men are not those that have the most money or
even the most brains. They are the men who
love and touch humanity with the deepest sympathy and affection. These are the men that

never die. They live with an impersonal immortality in this world as well as a personal immortality in the world beyond.

There was a time when we were prone to judge a man's religion by his negative conduct, by what he did not do. If he did not lie nor steal, nor drink, nor commit adultery, if he did not commit any serious breach of ethics, we felt he must be a Christian. But we discovered this method of investigation was faulty. Many a merchant is dishonest at heart while he is correct in his business life. His business conduct is good, not because he wants to do right, but because he understands full well that bad business methods would wreck his organization. Then we judged people by what they did. If they went to church and paid the budget and supported the interests of good citizenship and good morals, we felt that they must be Christians. But we discovered the fact that some men would join a church in order to help their business. If they were doctors or lawyers, they felt that the respectability and the social prestige that the church would throw round about them would increase their business, and consequently their income. It has been discovered that men living privately impure lives have redoubled their public efforts in the church, seemingly in order to cover up suspicion that they were inwardly impure. This method also failed. But there is one test that is infallible. Observe a man or woman under great pressure. Watch him with scrutiny when his will is crossed and his ambitions are thwarted and his desires are disappointed. The quality of spirit that he possesses at such times will determine the right or wrong of the man's inner life and character. One man said he could get along with anybody as long as he could have his own way. How remarkable! Who could not keep sweet and who could not be agreeable as long as his every desire and wish were granted? The test comes when we have to yield our will and surrender our desires and abandon our wishes to make others happy. There is no power in the world known to man that can enable us to do this gracefully except the power of the living God in the human soul. A Christian with a pure heart, full of divine love can be sweet in his heart when he can not have his way. He can yield his will and still be happy. He can set aside his own ambitions in the interest of others and for the promotion of God's cause and rejoice in his own loss while he sees the gain of others.

This is the test: the test of the spirit. Are we kind? Do we suffer long? Are we Christlike? Is the spirit like the spirit of Christ in the midst of the pressure and the sorrow and the losses and the anguish of this life?

It is common to hear people pray for more power, to pray for more fire, to pray for more joy. But it is uncommon indeed to hear people praying that they might possess the spirit of the Master; that they might be able to go the second mile of their own accord after having been compelled by others to go the first mile. Christ impressed the world by having that force of character to endure and suffer uncomplainingly. When they reviled Him, He reviled not again. When they struck Him, He did not hit back. He stood, He endured, He was patient, He was kind, He was immovable. What an example He has set for you and for me and we should want to be like Him in spirit that we too might stand firm and immovable in the face of Satanic attacks, and yet be kind, tender, sweet, and longsuffering under the lash and scourge of unkind treatment from others.

In this way we become the advertisers of Jesus Christ, for the world knows that no man can feel kindly toward others naturally when he is mistreated. To love your enemies is not human—that is divine. To keep sweet under mistreatment is not natural—that is supernatural.

Be thou therefore an example of the believer in spirit.

In an eastern city lived one of the greatest preachers of his generation. One day walking down the streets of that city were his daughter and a young lady friend of hers. These two were conversing about religion. The daughter of this eminent preacher remarked that when she traveled she always wanted to ride by the side of her father, for she felt if the train wrecked, the hand of protection and of providence that would be over her father's head would perchance protect her also. Her friend, deeply interested in the great confidence she manifested in her own father, asked why she felt as she did. The young lady replied that she had lived in the home of her father for nineteen years and during that time she had never known him to get out of humor, to speak an uncharitable word to her mother or to the children in the home. When he punished the children in the exercise of his governmental authority he always did so with a heart full of kindness, compassion and love, and she said the spirit her father manifested, the spirit of grief over disobedience, hurt the children more than his punishment. She said, "My father preached holiness and possessed the bless-

ing. He preached Christ's likeness and repro-
duced it in his own spirit."

What a legacy to leave a child. Far more
valuable is the memory of a spirit like that than
to inherit wealth, fortune or social prestige.
There is nothing so glorious as a thought of a
child beating a path to the grave of a parent and
there looking down upon the resting place of a
father or a mother with a memory of a clean,
spotless, upright life and a Christlike spirit.
This is an inheritance to which every child in the
world has a right. Christ Jesus our Lord can
work such a spirit in the heart of a man or a
woman that can be lived before others.

Fifth. Paul exhorts us to be examples of
the believers, or advertisers of Christ, in faith.
Faith is "Believing what God says, and believing
it because God says it." This is a simple definition but true nevertheless. Faith is believing
something, not because we feel it nor because we
want it, but believing it because God says it.
Again, one has said that faith comes from three
Hebrew root words. First, a word that means
persuasion; second, a word that means obedience; and third, one that when translated means
trust. Thus faith is constituted of three elements—persuasion, obedience, and trust. The
devil had the first element, namely, persuasion.

He met the Lord in the road, recognized that he faced his master, that he was conquered, and that there would be an end to his dominion. He trembled, he believed. He did not obey Christ nor trust Christ, but he was persuaded that he had met his master. Many people join the church with nothing but persuasion. They have been persuaded that sin was wrong, that the church was right; that they should be baptized and keep the ordinances, and that they should go to heaven; and finally, they have been persuaded to come forward and give the preacher their hand. But persuasion that Christ is able to save and that sin is wrong does not necessarily result in salvation. Thousands of sinners have the background of persuasion, but that is as far as they ever get. They will come out to church and support the institutions of the church because of the respect and confidence they have in the cause of truth, but persuasion never saves a man.

He must have the second element, namely, obedience. He must not only be persuaded that Christ is true, but he must consent to obey Christ by forsaking his sins and accepting the merits of the atonement. No man can pray, no man can trust, no man can believe, no man can be saved until he consents to perfectly obey the will of God. He must say "Yes."

But salvation will not result from persuasion and obedience alone, and they are only two of the elements in faith. There must be that perfect trust and commitment to the will of God demanded of us by the Bible. For example, a man may be persuaded that an airship could take him from one city to another. He might examine the propeller and the motor and the materials in the wings of the ship and be convinced perfectly in his own mind that the officer in charge and the ship under consideration are entirely capable of conveying him through space, but that is not sufficient. If he is to arrive he must obey the orders of the man in charge of the airship. He must put his foot on the step and climb into the ship. He must sit where he is told and he must consent to keep his hands off the instruments within that ship. He must do as he is told to do in perfect obedience to orders. Otherwise he would never get in; and if he did get in he might wreck the ship by his acts of disobedience to reasonable orders. But this would not be sufficient. He must trust the aviator. After he has been persuaded of the ability of the ship to carry him and of the aviator to operate the machinery and after he has consented to obey and does obey all orders, he must then trust himself, his life, his wife and children, his all in the hands of the aviator. This is faith. First he is persuaded, second he obeys, and third he trusts. Every Christian that enters life for Christ and His cause should be full of faith. He should be persuaded of the ability of Jesus Christ to carry him through every difficult place, and he should be willing to obey perfectly every order that Christ gives, and third, he should trust the Lord with all of his heart to carry him through.

Doubters have never succeeded as soldiers or business men or professional men. In business or professional life it is the man with confidence and faith that accomplishes results. God knows full well that His people can never inspire others to make the battle for heaven unless they are full of faith themselves. Confidence inspires faith; fear is catching. Faith is one of the most contagious things known. He that would advertise the kingdom of God must be an example of faith.

Sixth. Paul exhorts us to advertise Christ by being an example of the believer in purity. Here he points once more at the nature of man. Righteousness is the foundation of the kingdom of God, then comes joy and peace. Without righteousness there could be no peace nor could there be joy. Every house must have a proper foundation. Righteousness, moral integrity, are indispensable in the building of life and manhood.

The importance of purity is often overlooked. Many people seem to think that if they can have some great demonstration, some great gift, power, or fire, the ability to speak in some unknown tongue, or to perform some miracle that would distinguish them, they could then attract the world to Jesus Christ. But how many times have we found people with characteristics that they considered to be very attractive who would immediately resent the demands of heart purity and perfect love.

The church needs powerful Christians; it needs hot Christians, those that pray with a fervent spirit. The church needs Christians full of peace and joy. But the outstanding need is purity—purity of mind, purity of word, purity of spirit, purity of character, purity of life. Give us multitudes of men and women who are so upright, clean, and pure in their hearts, their morals, and in their characters that no just charge can be laid against them by even their bitterest enemies.

A man guilty of sin covered is weak. His conscience haunts him day and night, and the fear of ultimate exposure hangs over his head like a pall of death. Moments of peace are brief and are soon supplanted by pangs of fear and terror. The innocent man is the brave and the courageous man. He has no fear of exposure because he has done no wrong. His conscience is innocent and void of offense toward God and man. The strongest person in the world is the pure person. Purity is invulnerable, it is impregnable, it is indestructible from without. It can be destroyed only by consent of the ego within us. No nation has ever been crushed by external forces. The civilizations and the nations that have gone down have perished from within. The vital forces of national life, the inner powers of resistance and progress have perished and then the forces that came upon them that were external crushed them like an egg shell. No man can justly claim to have been ruined by some force outside of himself. The man or woman who is pure in heart with pure motives, pure thoughts, pure intentions, pure affections and a will set on doing right, is absolutely indestructible.

The world contaminated with sin and moral leprosy is unconsciously looking for purity of heart and character that will exemplify Jesus Christ and will make proof of His cleansing. The

Lord announced that He came to the world to destroy the works of the devil. Can He do it? And has He done it? Where is the evidence? Who can show the product? Who can give the proof? Where is that man or woman that has a pure heart and a pure life, that can stand out in the midst of smut and dirt, in the midst of a crooked and perverse generation, without spot and blemish? If God can put within the heart of the lily the power to expel the soot and dust that would accumulate on its white face, He can certainly put within the heart of man a power that can throw off the contaminating moral smut and pollution of a sinful environment. Who has seen the lily with its white face turned toward the sun covered with soot falling from a smoke-stack of the great factory? The lily looked as if it were ruined, hopelessly ruined, but the first breeze that blew over the lily lifted from its white face the soot and the dirt and left it standing in its beautiful purity, untarnished. The nature that kept the smut from sticking to the lily had an expulsive force that God and nature put within it. Christ Jesus can take a man or a woman, remove all sin from the heart and put within that heart His own personality, a power that can enable such a person to live above reproach in the midst of a crooked and perverse generation. Purity of life is an essential in advertising Christians, the Bible, and the Christian's Savior.

Thousands of people have wept over the fact that they were not preachers or missionaries or otherwise public servants of Jesus Christ. What a mistake they have made to feel that their lives amount to nothing since they are not outstanding leaders. The greatest work that a man will ever do for Christ is not preaching, it is not singing, it is not giving his money, it is not sacrificing his very blood. His greatest contribution to Jesus Christ is living before the world a life that is above reproach, one that exemplifies the spirit and character of his Lord. His greatest work is in being a living advertiser that will make the world hungry for Christ and His gifts.

Every man is a credit to the cause of Christ or a discredit. He is an honor or he is a dishonor. He draws the world nearer to Christ or he tends to drive it away from Christ. Which are we doing?

We would be pleased to sum up the contents of this little book in one final word.

First. Holiness, an essential for heaven, is the work of God in the soul of man, taking out sin and putting within him the image of Christ. It is the removing of sin and the infilling of divine love.

Second. The ethics of holiness is man's work and is imperfect because of man's mental limitations and of his lack of experience and limited amount of knowledge.

Third. The objections to holiness are found not in the work of God in the heart, which is perfect and without fault, but in the ethics of men.

Fourth. We should differentiate between the experience of holiness, the work of God, and the ethics of holiness, the work of man, keeping in mind that one might have a perfect experience and yet not produce a perfect life.

Fifth. The importance of right ethics can not be overestimated, because the ethics of our life is what others see and will tend to bring them closer to God or cause them to discredit the claims of salvation.

Sixth. Every Christian is an advertiser for Jesus Christ and His kingdom, and should seek to improve his ethics in order that he might be an asset to Jesus Christ and His kingdom.

Seventh. We should rejoice over the perfect image of Christ within, the perfect ideal created in the human heart by the spirit of God, but we should deplore the defects in the ethics of our lives, and strive with prayer and holy passion to make our ethics commensurate with the glorious experience created within the human heart by the Holy Ghost.